A DEVOTIONAL

VOLUME 1

SANDRA WADE

LUCIDBOOKS

The Nearness of God
A Devotional, Volume 1

Copyright © 2019 by Sandra Wade

Published by Lucid Books in Houston, TX
www.LucidBooksPublishing.com

All rights reserved. No part of this publication may be reproduced, stored in a retrieval system, or transmitted in any form by any means, electronic, mechanical, photocopy, recording, or otherwise, without the prior permission of the publisher, except as provided for by USA copyright law.

Unless otherwise indicated, all Scripture quotations are taken from the New American Standard Bible® (NASB), Copyright © 1960, 1962, 1963, 1968, 1971, 1972, 1973, 1975, 1977, 1995 by The Lockman Foundation. Used by permission. www.Lockman.org.

Scripture quotations marked (ESV) are taken from the ESV® Bible (The Holy Bible, English Standard Version®), copyright © 2001 by Crossway, a publishing ministry of Good News Publishers. Used by permission. All rights reserved.

Scripture quotations marked (NLT) are taken from the Holy Bible, New Living Translation, copyright © 1996, 2004, 2007, 2013, 2015 by Tyndale House Foundation. Used by permission of Tyndale House Publishers, Inc., Carol Stream, Illinois 60188. All rights reserved.

Scripture quotations marked (NIV) are taken from the Holy Bible, New International Version®, NIV®. Copyright © 1973, 1978, 1984, 2011 by Biblica, Inc.™ Used by permission of Zondervan. All rights reserved worldwide. www.zondervan.com The "NIV" and "New International Version" are trademarks registered in the United States Patent and Trademark Office by Biblica, Inc.™

Scripture quotations marked (GNT) are taken from the Good News Bible © 1994 published by the Bible Societies/HarperCollins Publishers Ltd UK, Good News Bible © American Bible Society 1966, 1971, 1976, 1992. Used with permission.

ISBN-10: 1-63296-316-7 | ISBN-13: 978-1-63296-316-1
eISBN-10: 1-63296-283-7 | eISBN-13: 978-1-63296-283-6

Special Sales: Most Lucid Books titles are available in special quantity discounts. Custom imprinting or excerpting can also be done to fit special needs. Contact Lucid Books at Info@LucidBooksPublishing.com.

To: _____

From: _____

"But as for me, ***the nearness of God is my good***;
I have made the Lord God my refuge,
That I may tell of all Your works."

—Ps. 73:28

All words in reference to the deity of Christ are capitalized in honor of the respect and love I have for the Father, the Son, and the Holy Spirit, and I pray this capitalization aids the reader in the clarity of Whom I speak. I also will not acknowledge by capitalization "the enemy," the "evil one," "satan," lucifer, nor any reference to him, from the respect and love I have for my heavenly Father. I pray this aids the reader as to Whom is the King of kings and Lord of lords. Scripture translations are printed as is and have preserved the original capitalization within each version.

With love, Sandi

Contents

Introduction	1
Strength through Worship	3
The Holy Spirit: A Study	6
The Bible: The Word of God	10
God	12
Jesus Christ: The Son of God	14
Sin	18
Judgments	20
Rewards	23
The Church	27
Prayer: Part 1	33
Faith	37
The Abundant Life	43
Repentance	46
The New Birth	49
Paul's Farewell to Ephesus	52
Creation	56
Transformation	58
Walk in the Light	62
Daily Testing	64
The Church: Its Worship and Work	66
Make a Difference	69
Healing	71
Personal Changes	75
God's Word: Food for Thought	77
Love	87

Thorn in His Flesh	90
Putting the Thanks Back in Thanksgiving	93
Encouragement	95
Romans	98
Armor of God	99
Prophetic Movement	102
The Apostles' Creed	104
Prayer: Part 2	107

Special Thanks

First, I would like to thank God for loving me and holding me close to Him throughout my years on earth. Through good and bad, I have always been able to count on Him. I love Him first and foremost, and through His Son, my Savior Jesus the Messiah, I am saved and shall enjoy eternal life with Him.

I would like to thank God for placing my maternal grandmother, Canny, in my life. She was a lady of strong conviction and love for our Savior Jesus Christ and spoke His truth to me all my years with her. My first recollection of her introducing Jesus to me was when I was two years old. I recall the beautiful day, standing on the country wooden bridge by our home, looking across the field at a white horse, and seeing His light appear. As a child, everything seemed bright, clean, and sparkling. I can still see this in my mind's eye. My mother, amazed by my memory, talked with me about this and revealed to me my age. I am amazed by my heavenly Father's grace that saved a wretch like me. God's goodness is revealed to all those who seek to find Him.

I would like to thank my dear friend Mary Kay Freeman Falkner for asking me to write to her daughter some encouraging words of our Christian faith. This one request turned into years of walking with God and hearing His voice to write devotionals for the purpose of moving others toward Him as He so moved me. I thank God, my heavenly Father, my Savior and best friend Jesus Christ, and my Helper, His Holy Spirit, who guided me and gave me wisdom for His purpose. Without my Helper, this would not have been possible.

Introduction

The Nearness of God was not a book I set out to write. It began as regular e-mails sent to a friend's daughter to share my faith. Using my life experiences, I sought to focus on God and His Word, letting the Bible provide answers and solutions for her spiritual walk. Over time, the e-mails began to circulate among other friends until the number of readers grew and reached our church family, resulting in a place on our church's website.

The e-mails led me to research God's Word more deeply and thoroughly in order to have more insights to offer. I learned how to share my own burdens and experiences so others could find comfort and grow. That is God's purpose for me—to use my life experiences to connect scripture with examples for inspiration and guidance.

Now, more than five years later, I have a lengthy library of those weekly e-mails that groups are now using for devotionals, studies, and meditation. But the e-mails need to go beyond my computer and those groups. If God gave me those truths, I should make them more available.

Putting the e-mails into book form has allowed me to organize them for easier reference and study. Some issues don't always have easy answers, but I've learned that God always has answers for those who are willing to listen.

I hope you find your own connection and direction to the answers you're searching for. Sometimes, finding the answer biblically can be hard. I hope this resource will help you on your own journey.

Strength through Worship

But the time is coming—indeed it's here now—when true worshipers will worship the Father in spirit and in truth. The Father is looking for those who will worship him that way.
—John 4:23 NLT

When we worship on earth, we are in tune with heaven. Revelation gives us this description of worship in heaven:

And they sang in a mighty chorus: "Worthy is the Lamb who was slaughtered—to receive power and riches and wisdom and strength and honor and glory and blessing."
—Rev. 5:12 NLT

Worship helps us put our thoughts and issues into perspective. The psalmist Asaph asked the age-old question: *Why do the wicked prosper?* His answer came when he communed with God.

Then I went into your sanctuary, O God,
  and I finally understood the destiny of the wicked.
Truly, you put them on a slippery path
  and send them sliding over the cliff to destruction.
—Ps. 73:17–18 NLT

Sometimes we don't understand why things are the way they are, but when we come and worship, when we hear the Word of God, we gain perspective. When the end of the week arrives, many eagerly go to church to hear news that will bring peace and calm for the soul.

We can become weak from stress, family disturbances, disease, upheavals, devastating news, or persecution from others. Christians must turn to Jesus who strengthens. People may say our faith is strong, but what they see is not our faith but Christ's grace and strength through us. We need His help. We need fellow Christians. We need Bible studies. We need a place set aside to worship our heavenly Father. God is in our presence when we gather as two or more in His name. We have a big God, and what is impossible for humans is possible with Him when we allow Him to work in our lives.

> *And let us consider how to stir up one another to love and good works, not neglecting to meet together, as is the habit of some, but encouraging one another, and all the more as you see the Day drawing near.*
> —Heb. 10:24–25 ESV

> *What then, brothers? When you come together, each one has a hymn, a lesson, a revelation, a tongue, or an interpretation. Let all things be done for building up.*
> —1 Cor. 14:26 ESV

> *Let the word of Christ dwell in you richly, teaching and admonishing one another in all wisdom, singing psalms and hymns and spiritual songs, with thankfulness in your hearts to God.*
> —Col. 3:16 ESV

> *For where two or three are gathered in my name, there am I among them.*
> —Matt. 18:20 ESV

> *Whoever is not with me is against me, and whoever does not gather with me scatters.*
> —Matt. 12:30 ESV

> *Therefore encourage one another and build one another up, just as you are doing.*
> —1 Thess. 5:11 ESV

When we are praising the Lord on earth, we are joining the chorus of heaven. The angels stand before Him singing, "Holy, Holy, Art Thou God Almighty." God is looking for people to worship Him in spirit and in truth. Worshipping God in church is healing to our souls, prepares us for the days ahead, encourages us to study, and urges us to gather frequently, giving thanks to Him for and in all things.

> *Do not quench the Spirit; do not despise prophetic utterances. But examine everything carefully; hold fast to that which is good; abstain from every form of evil.*
>
> —1Thess. 5:19–22

The Holy Spirit: A Study

The Holy Spirit is God, equal to the Father and the Son. Don't ever speak of Him as *it* or refer to Him as *an influence*. He is God the Holy Spirit, set forth in the Bible as distinct from the Father and the Son while equal in status. In Genesis, the Holy Spirit is actively engaged with the Father and the Son in the work of creation:

> *In the beginning God created the heavens and the earth. The earth was formless and void, and darkness was over the surface of the deep; and the Spirit of God was moving over the surface of the waters.*
> —Gen. 1:1–2 emphasis added

This scripture reveals God as Spirit. In the Old Testament, the Holy Spirit empowered people for service, but when they were disobedient, He departed from them. When David sinned against the Lord, he prayed, *"Do not take Your Holy Spirit from me"* (Ps. 51:11).

In the New Testament, the Holy Spirit came at Pentecost and indwelled believers permanently, filling and empowering them and all who've since believed. The study of the person and work of the Holy Spirit is of utmost importance because He will make you a better Christian and servant of God.

1. The Deity of the Holy Spirit

But Peter said, "Ananias, why has Satan filled your heart to lie to the Holy Spirit *and to keep back some of the price of the land? While it remained unsold, did it not remain your own? And after it was sold, was it not under your control? Why is it that you have conceived this deed in your heart? You have not lied to men but to God."*

—Acts 5:3–4 emphasis added

Here, Peter reveals that Ananias lied to the Holy Spirit, who is also shown to be God in the last sentence, revealing that God and the Holy Spirit are one.

2. The Emblems of the Holy Spirit

John answered and said to them all, "As for me, I baptize you with water; but One is coming who is mightier than I, and I am not fit to untie the thong of His sandals; He will baptize you with the Holy Spirit and fire."

—Luke 3:16 emphasis added

John is referring to Jesus as the One. In Acts 1:5, Jesus said, *"For John baptized with water, but you will be baptized with the Holy Spirit not many days from now."* That revealed that as water washes the filth from our flesh, cleansing and purifying us, God in His Spirit would reside within us to cleanse and purify the hearts of those who believe. That is a good result, a blessing from God, to give believers a Helper on their journeys. Jesus also baptized with fire. The Holy Spirit worked as fire, purging them and burning up their lusts and corrupt desires. The flame of purification is seen in Isaiah 6:6–7:

Then one of the seraphim flew to me with a burning coal in his hand, which he had taken from the altar with tongs. He touched my mouth with it and said, "Behold, this has touched your lips; and your iniquity is taken away and your sin is forgiven."

3. Sins against the Holy Spirit

Therefore I say to you, any sin and blasphemy shall be forgiven people, but blasphemy against the Spirit shall not be forgiven. *Whoever speaks a word against the Son of Man, it shall be forgiven him; but whoever speaks against the Holy Spirit, it shall not be forgiven him, either in this age, or in the age to come.*

—Matt. 12:31–32 emphasis added

God is the Holy Spirit, and Jesus was born of His Spirit. If we deny the Spirit, we also deny God and His Son, our Savior. Is it possible for a believer to blaspheme the Holy Ghost? A true believer holds fast to the written Word of God and knows the Helper, the Holy Spirit, who resides within him or her, guides, and directs. The Spirit connects believers to God through Jesus Christ. The Pharisee Saul who blasphemed Jesus received God's mercy when he repented and was baptized and filled with the Holy Spirit. He became a true believer in Jesus, the Son of God, the risen Lord, and Savior of the world. Saul's sins were forgiven, and he walked in the Spirit henceforth, becoming a faithful believer, the apostle Paul, an evangelist, and the author of many books of the Bible. Blasphemous words against the Holy Spirit will not be forgiven as the words reveal the true treasury of the heart. A blasphemous tongue against the Holy Spirit condemns and reveals the unbelieving self. Only true believers are redeemed and forgiven of their sins.

4. The Work of the Holy Spirit

But I [Jesus Christ] tell you the truth, it is to your advantage that I go away; for if I do not go away, the Helper will not come to you; but if I go, I will send Him to you. And He, when He comes, will convict the world concerning sin and righteousness and judgment; concerning sin, because they do not believe in Me; and concerning righteousness, because I go to the Father and you no longer see Me; and concerning judgment, because the ruler of this world has been judged.

I have many more things to say to you, but you cannot bear them now. But when He, the Spirit of Truth, comes, He will guide you into all the truth; for He will not speak on His own initiative, but whatever He hears, He will speak; and He will disclose to you what is to come. He will glorify Me, for He will take of Mine and will disclose it to you. All things that the Father has are Mine; therefore I said that He takes of Mine and will disclose it to you.

—John 16:7–15

5. The Fruit of the Holy Spirit

But the fruit of the Spirit *is love, joy, peace, patience, kindness, goodness, faithfulness, gentleness, self-control; against such things there is no law.*

—Gal. 5:22–23 emphasis added

When we walk in the Spirit, His character will be seen through us, and there is no law against the goodness of His Spirit.

The Bible: The Word of God

Because it's so important for a Christian to start on the right foundation, you must establish your faith in the Bible, for it is the Word of God.

The Bible is not a book of philosophy, although it is philosophical in the sense that the Bible is devoted to the study of the fundamental nature of knowledge, reality, and existence, enabled by the Holy Spirit to reveal a calm attitude toward disappointments or difficulties. It is not scientific, although there is no discrepancy between ascertained facts of science and the Bible. It is not a book of history, but it contains an accurate historical record. The Bible was given to people from God and God the Son, the only Savior. *"Jesus said to him, 'I am the way, and the truth, and the life; no one comes to the Father but through Me"* (John 14:6).

The Word of God is the great book of instruction with examples for an abundant life on earth. From Genesis to Revelation, God spares no detail of the quality life we may have. The Bible is not a means of eternal life, but it is the means to come to know His Son, our Savior Jesus Christ, who is the only means to the Father for eternal life. Jesus said, *"You search the Scriptures because you think that in them you have eternal life; it is these that testify about Me; and you are unwilling to come to Me so that you may have life"* (John 5:39–40).

As the heavens are above the earth, so is the Bible higher than all other books. Inside each Bible distributed by the Gideons

The Bible: The Word of God

International are these words: "Read it to be wise, believe it to be safe, and practice it to be holy."[1]

1. The Bible Is the Inspired Word of God

All Scripture is inspired by God and profitable for teaching, for reproof, for correction, for training in righteousness; so that the man of God may be adequate, equipped for every good work.

—2 Tim. 3:16–17 emphasis added

2. The Bible Is a Difficult Book

But a natural man does not accept the things of the Spirit of God, for they are foolishness to him; and he cannot understand them, because they are spiritually appraised. But he who is spiritual appraises all things, yet he himself is appraised by no one. For WHO HAS KNOWN THE MIND OF THE LORD, THAT HE WILL INSTRUCT HIM? *But we have the mind of Christ.*

—1 Cor. 2:14–16 emphasis added

3. The Bible Is a Book of Oneness

For no prophecy was ever made by an act of human will, but men moved by the Holy Spirit spoke from God.

—2 Pet. 1:21

4. The Bible Claims Special Power

For the word of God is living and active and sharper than any two-edged sword, and piercing as far as the division of soul and spirit, of both joints and marrow, and able to judge the thoughts and intentions of the heart.

—Heb. 4:12

5. The Bible Commands Believers to Study It

Be diligent to present yourself approved to God as a workman who does not need to be ashamed, accurately handling the word of truth.

—2 Tim. 2:15

---

1. The Gideons International, "An Inspiring Introduction to the Holy Book," December 31, 2010, http://blog.gideons.org/2010/12/the-bible-contains-the-mind-of-god/.

God

The Bible reveals God as the only infinite and eternal being, having no beginning and no ending. He is the creator and sustainer of all things, the supreme personal intelligence and righteous ruler of the universe. He is life and therefore the only source of life. Jesus said, *"For just as the Father has life in Himself, even so He gave to the Son also to have life in Himself"* (John 5:26).

Humans are natural and cannot know God by their own wisdom. Job asked, *"Can you discover the depths of God?"* (Job 11:7). God is a person and can be known only by revelation. In the Old Testament, He revealed Himself to and through His prophets. In the New Testament, He revealed Himself through His Son, Jesus Christ:

> *God, after He spoke long ago to the fathers in the prophets in many portions and in many ways, in these last days has spoken to us in His Son, whom He appointed heir of all things, through whom also He made the world. And He is the radiance of His glory and the exact representation of His nature, and upholds all things by the word of His power. When He had made purification of sins, He sat down at the right hand of the Majesty on high, having become as much better than the angels, as He has inherited a more excellent name than they.*
> —Heb. 1:1–4

1. The Existence of God

By faith Enoch was taken up so that he would not see death; AND HE WAS NOT FOUND BECAUSE GOD TOOK HIM UP; *for he obtained the witness that before his being taken up he was pleasing to God.*

2. Christ's Humanity

Concerning His Son, Who was born of a descendant of David according to the flesh, who was declared the Son of God with power by the resurrection from the dead, according to the Spirit of holiness, Jesus Christ our Lord.

—Rom. 1:3–4

3. Christ's Virgin Birth

Now in the sixth month the angel Gabriel was sent from God to a city in Galilee called Nazareth, to a virgin engaged to a man whose name was Joseph, of the descendants of David; and the virgin's name was Mary. And coming in, he said to her, "Greetings, favored one! The Lord is with you." But she was very perplexed at this statement, and kept pondering what kind of salutation this was. The angel said to her, "Do not be afraid, Mary; for you have found favor with God. And behold, you will conceive in your womb and bear a son, and you shall name Him Jesus. He will be great and will be called the Son of the Most High; and the Lord God will give Him the throne of His father David; and He will reign over the house of Jacob forever, and His kingdom will have no end." Mary said to the angel, "How can this be, since I am a virgin?" The angel answered and said to her, "The Holy Spirit will come upon you, and the power of the Most High will overshadow you; and for that reason the holy Child shall be called the Son of God.

—Luke 1:26–35

4. Christ's Death

And being found in appearance as a man, He humbled Himself by becoming obedient to the point of death, even death on a cross.

—Phil. 2:8

5. Christ's Resurrection

He is Risen! *After the Sabbath, at dawn on the first day of the week, Mary Magdalene and the other Mary went to look at the tomb.*

There was a violent earthquake, for an angel of the Lord came down from heaven and, going to the tomb, rolled back the stone and sat on it. His appearance was like lightning, and his clothes were white as snow. The guards were so afraid of him that they shook and became like dead men.

The angel said to the women, "Do not be afraid, for I know that you are looking for Jesus, who was crucified. He is not here; he has risen, just as he said. Come and see the place where he lay. Then go quickly and tell his disciples: 'He has risen from the dead and is going ahead of you into Galilee. There you will see him.' Now I have told you."

So the women hurried away from the tomb, afraid yet filled with joy, and ran to tell his disciples. Suddenly Jesus met them. "Greetings," he said. They came to him, clasped his feet and worshiped him. Then Jesus said to them, "Do not be afraid. Go and tell my brothers to go to Galilee; there they will see me."

—Matt. 28:1–10 NIV

The Guards' Report

While the women were on their way, some of the guards went into the city and reported to the chief priests everything that had happened. When the chief priests had met with the elders and devised a plan, they gave the soldiers a large sum of money, telling them, "You are to say, 'His disciples came during the night and stole him away while we were asleep.' If this report gets to the governor, we will satisfy him and keep you out of trouble." So the soldiers took the money and did as they were instructed. And this story has been widely circulated among the Jews to this very day.

—Matt. 28:11–15 NIV

The Great Commission

Then the eleven disciples went to Galilee, to the mountain where Jesus had told them to go. When they saw him, they worshiped him; but some doubted. Then Jesus came to them and said, "All authority in heaven and on earth has been given to me. Therefore go and make disciples of all nations, baptizing them in the name of the Father and of the Son and of the Holy Spirit, and teaching them to obey everything I have commanded you. And surely I am with you always, to the very end of the age."

—Matt. 28:16–20 NIV

6. Christ's Ascension and Second Coming

And after He had said these things, He was lifted up while they were looking on, and a cloud received Him out of their sight. And as they were gazing intently into the sky while He was going, behold, two men in white clothing stood beside them. They also said, "Men of Galilee, why do you stand looking into the sky? This Jesus, who has been taken up from you into heaven, will come in just the same way as you have watched Him go into heaven."

—Acts 1:9–11

Every day is a celebration of Christ's death and resurrection. Without His death, we would be eternally dead. When we realize that we are dead without Him, we should be humbled, filled with gratitude, and urged to spread the good news of the gospel. Those who believe that Jesus is Christ, the risen Lord and Savior, will have eternal life. Spread this news! Accepting Christ as Savior and sharing that good news with others are the most important acts of our lives.

Sin

Sin often results in two startling facts. The first fact is that humans often think little of it or consider it an illusion, a religious mirage, or the invention of fanatics. Many deny, joke about, or laugh at it. Others acknowledge it, but it has no bearing on their lives. They continue in sin with little thought of its penalty.

The second fact is that God thinks much of sin. He said, *"The person who sins will die"* (Ezek. 18:20), and *"The wages of sin is death"* (Rom. 6:23). All sins are an abomination to God (Prov. 6:16-19), and He hates those who do iniquity (Ps. 5:5).

Moses said, *"Everyone who acts unjustly is an abomination to the* LORD*"* (Deut. 25:16). Sin is an evil force. We cannot escape it in this life, but we can overcome it by the power of God.

1. The Origin of Sin

And angels who did not keep their own domain, but abandoned their proper abode, He has kept in eternal bonds under darkness for the judgment of the great day.

—Jude 1:6

2. The Definition of Sin

Everyone who practices sin also practices lawlessness; and sin is lawlessness.

—1 John 3:4

3. The Entrance of Sin

Therefore, just as through one man sin entered into the world, and death through sin, and so death spread to all men, because all sinned.

—Rom. 5:12

4. The Results of Sin

And you were dead in your trespasses and sins.

—Eph. 2:1

5. God's Remedy for Sin

We beg you on behalf of Christ, be reconciled to God.

—2 Cor. 5:20

He made Him [Jesus Christ] who knew no sin to be sin on our behalf, so that we might become the righteousness of God in Him.

—2 Cor. 5:21

Jesus Christ gives us life eternal. When we reflect on all our Savior endured so we could live an abundant life (John 10:10), we should be humbled, grateful, and awed. We must seek Him daily and ask the Holy Spirit to keep our sins before our eyes, for only when we repent and renew our minds in His Word can we please our heavenly Father.

Judgments

In 2 Timothy 2:15, we are told, *"Be diligent to present yourself approved to God as a workman who does not need to be ashamed, accurately handling the word of truth."*

Don't try to make all judgments conform to one general judgment. The general judgment theory stems from religious invention, not the Word of God. The Bible reveals five judgments, and they differ in time, place, and purpose. However, they all have one thing in common: the Lord Jesus Christ is the judge. *"For not even the Father judges anyone, but He has given all judgment to the Son"* (John 5:22). Everyone—from Adam to the last person born—will stand before the Lord Jesus Christ to be judged.

1. In the first judgment, the sins of believers have already been judged in Christ on the cross.

Truly, truly, I say to you, he who hears My word, and believes Him who sent Me, has eternal life, and does not come into judgment, but has passed out of death into life.

—John 5:24

2. In the second judgment, the believer must judge himself or herself, or the Lord Jesus Christ will judge and discipline him or her.

But if we judged ourselves rightly, we should not be judged. But when we are judged, we are disciplined by the Lord so that we will not be condemned along with the world.

—1 Cor. 11:31–32

3. In the third judgment, all believers appear before the judgment seat of Christ, where their works are judged.

For we must all appear before the judgment seat of Christ, so that each one may be recompensed for his deeds in the body, according to what he has done, whether good or bad.

—2 Cor. 5:10

4. In the fourth judgment, all nations are judged at the second coming of Christ.

But when the Son of Man comes in His glory, and all the angels with Him, then He will sit on His glorious throne. All the nations will be gathered before Him; and He will separate them from one another, as the shepherd separates the sheep from the goats; and He will put the sheep on His right, and the goats on the left.

Then the King will say to those on His right, "Come, you who are blessed of My Father, inherit the kingdom prepared for you from the foundation of the world. For I was hungry, and you gave Me something to eat; I was thirsty, and you gave Me something to drink; I was a stranger, and you invited Me in; naked, and you clothed Me; I was sick, and you visited Me; I was in prison, and you came to Me." Then the righteous will answer Him, "Lord, when did we see You hungry, and feed You, or thirsty, and give You something to drink? And when did we see You a stranger, and invite You in, or naked, and clothe You? When did we see You sick, or in prison, and come to You?" The King will answer and say to them, "Truly I say to you, to the extent that you did it to one of these brothers of Mine, even the least of them, you did it to Me."

Then He will also say to those on His left, "Depart from Me, accursed ones, into the eternal fire which has been prepared for the devil and his angels; for I was hungry, and you gave Me nothing to eat; I was thirsty, and you gave Me nothing to drink; I was a stranger, and you did not invite Me in; naked, and you did not clothe Me; sick, and in prison, and you did not visit Me." Then they themselves also will answer, "Lord, when did we see You hungry, or thirsty, or a stranger, or naked, or sick, or in prison, and did not take care of You?" Then He will answer them, "Truly I say to you, to the extent that you did not do it to one of the least of these, you did not do it to Me." These will go away into eternal punishment, but the righteous into eternal life.

—Matt. 25:31–46

5. In the fifth judgment, the wicked dead are judged at the great white throne.

Then I saw a great white throne and Him who sat upon it, from whose presence earth and heaven fled away, and no place was found for them. And I saw the dead, the great and the small, standing before the throne, and books were opened; and another book was opened, which is the book of life; and the dead were judged from the things which were written in the books, according to their deeds. And the sea gave up the dead which were in it, and death and Hades gave up the dead which were in them; and they were judged, every one of them according to their deeds. Then death and Hades were thrown into the lake of fire. This is the second death, the lake of fire. And if anyone's name was not found written in the book of life, he was thrown into the lake of fire.

—Rev. 20:11–15

May the Word of God enhance our celebration of the risen Lord Jesus Christ, giving thanks for our liberty through Him, and cause unbelievers to repent and believe.

Rewards

There's a vast difference between the doctrine of salvation for the lost and the doctrine of rewards for the saved. Salvation is the gift of God. *"For by grace you have been saved through faith; and that not of yourselves, it is the gift of God; not as a result of works, so that no one may boast"* (Eph. 2:8–9, emphasis added).

Salvation is received by faith in the finished work of the Lord Jesus Christ. *"He who believes in the Son has eternal life; but he who does not obey the Son will not see life, but the wrath of God abides on him"* (John 3:36).

God rewards the works of believers. *"For the Son of Man is going to come in the glory of His Father with His angels, and* WILL THEN REPAY EVERY MAN ACCORDING TO HIS DEEDS*"* (Matt. 16:27 emphasis added).

Paul made the most revealing reference to rewards in 1 Corinthians 3:8–15:

> *Now he who plants and he who waters are one; but each will receive his own reward according to his own labor. For we are God's fellow workers; you are God's field, God's building.*
>
> *According to the grace of God which was given to me, as a wise master builder I laid a foundation, and another is building on it. But each man must be careful how he builds on it. For no man can lay a foundation other than the one which is laid, which is Jesus Christ. Now if any man builds on the foundation with gold, silver, precious stones, wood, hay, straw, each man's work will become evident; for the day will show it because it is to be revealed with fire, and the fire itself will test the quality each man's work. If any man's work*

which he has built on it remains, he will receive a reward. If any man's work is burned up, he will suffer loss; but he himself will be saved, yet so as through fire.

Here are the key takeaways:
1. Every believer will be rewarded *"according to his own labor"* (verse 8), but we do not labor for salvation to become believers.
2. *"We are God's fellow workers"* (verse 9), not for salvation, but for rewards.
3. The believer is not to build *"a foundation other than the one which is laid, which is Jesus Christ"* (verse 11).
4. The believer can choose two building materials: eternal (gold, silver, and precious stones) or temporal (wood, hay, straw) (verse 12).

While we look not at the things which are seen, but at the things which are not seen; for the things which are seen are temporal, but the things which are not seen are eternal.

—2 Cor. 4:18

The believer who builds on Christ with eternal materials—gold, silver, precious stones—shall receive a reward. Those who build on Christ with temporal materials—wood, hay, straw—will receive no reward. The temporal works will be destroyed at the Judgment Seat of Christ, and the believer will suffer loss—not the loss of salvation, but the loss of eternal rewards.

Some believers will be ashamed at the Judgment Seat of Christ because their works were temporal. *"Now, little children, abide in Him, so that when He appears, we may have confidence and not shrink away from Him in shame at His coming"* (1 John 2:28).

When you die, will you be afraid and ashamed to face Jesus? Will you face Him empty-handed because you lived for self, building your life on wood, hay, and straw?

Rewards are called crowns or wreaths in the New Testament.

Rewards

1. The Crown of Life

Blessed is a man who perseveres under trial; for once he has been approved, he will receive the crown of life which the Lord *has promised to those who love Him.*

—James 1:12

2. The Wreath Imperishable

Do you not know that those who run in a race all run, but only one receives the prize? Run in such a way that you may win. Everyone who competes in the games exercises self-control in all things. They then do it to receive a perishable wreath, but we an imperishable. Therefore I run in such a way, as not without aim; I box in such a way, as not beating the air; but I discipline my body and make it my slave, so that, after I have preached to others, I myself will not be disqualified.

—1 Cor. 9:24–27

3. The Crown of Exultation

For who is our hope or joy or crown of exultation? Is it not even you, in the presence of our Lord Jesus at His coming? For you are our glory and joy.

—1 Thess. 2:19–20

4. The Crown of Righteousness

But you, be sober in all things, endure hardship, do the work of an evangelist, fulfill your ministry.

For I am already being poured out as a drink offering, and the time of my departure has come. I have fought the good fight, I have finished the course, I have kept the faith; in the future there is laid up for me the crown of righteousness, which the Lord, the righteous Judge, will award to me on that day; and not only to me, but also to all who have loved His appearing.

—2 Tim. 4:5–8 emphasis added

5. The Crown of Glory

Shepherd the flock of God among you, exercising oversight not under compulsion, but voluntarily, according to the will of God; and not for sordid gain, but with eagerness; nor yet as lording it over those allotted to your charge, but proving to be examples to the flock. And when the Chief Shepherd appears, you will receive the unfading crown of glory.
—1 Pet. 5:2–4 emphasis added (see also 1 Pet. 5:6–14)

Seek the Holy Spirit for guidance in the direction of service that God has for you, according to His will, with kindness, love, gentleness, and a joyful spirit. The Lord finds much pleasure from those serving with a loving and joyful heart, and His reward is just.

The Church

Jesus said, *"And upon this rock I will build My church; and the gates of Hades will not overpower it"* (Matt. 16:18). The Greek word *ecclesia* in the New Testament designates any assembly or congregation, whether political (Acts 19:39), Christian (Eph. 1:22–23), or national (Acts 7:38). God called Israel out of Egypt, and they congregated in the wilderness. They were the church in the wilderness.

Today, God calls believers to congregate in worship—the church *in* the world but not *of* it. Unlike the church in the wilderness, the church that Jesus is building will never cease. Jesus said, *"The gates of Hades shall not overpower it"* (Matt. 16:18). His church

> *is built on the foundation of the apostles and prophets, Christ Jesus himself being the cornerstone, in whom the whole structure, being joined together, grows into a holy temple in the Lord. In Him you also are being built together into a dwelling place for God by the Spirit.*
> —Eph. 2:20–22 ESV

Beware of those who profess to be Christians but don't know Christ as their personal Savior:

> *Not everyone who says to Me, "Lord, Lord," will enter the kingdom of heaven, but he who does the will of My Father who is in heaven will enter. Many will say to Me on that day, "Lord, Lord, did we not prophesy in Your name, and in Your name cast out demons, and in Your name perform many miracles?" And then I will declare to*

them, *"I never knew you;* depart from Me, you who practice lawlessness.*"*

—Matt. 7:21–23

[They are] holding to a form of godliness, although they have denied its power; Avoid such men as these.

—2 Tim. 3:5

They profess to know God, but by their deeds they deny Him, being detestable and disobedient and worthless for any good deed.

—Titus 1:16

Only blood-washed, born-again, Spirit-baptized believers establish His church, which Jesus is actively building. The Bible contains much information about the church of Christ:

1. It's a Mystery

That by revelation there was made known to me the mystery, as I wrote before in brief. By referring to this, when you read you can understand my insight into the mystery of Christ, which in other generations was not made known to the sons of men, as it has now been revealed to His holy apostles and prophets in the Spirit; to be specific, that the Gentiles are fellow heirs and fellow members of the body, and fellow partakers of the promise in Christ Jesus through the gospel, of which I was made a minister, according to the gift of God's grace which was given to me according to the working of His power. To me, the very least of all saints, this grace was given, to preach to the Gentiles the unfathomable riches of Christ, and to bring to light what is the administration of the mystery which for ages has been hidden in God who created all things; so that the manifold wisdom of God might now be made known through the church to the rulers and the authorities in the heavenly places.

—Eph. 3:3–10

2. It's a Body

For even as the body is one and yet has many members, and all the members of the body, though they are many, are one body, so

The Church

also is Christ. For by one Spirit we were all baptized into one body, whether Jews or Greeks, whether slaves or free, and we were all made to drink of one Spirit.

For the body is not one member, but many. If the foot says, "Because I am not a hand, I am not a part of the body," it is not for this reason any the less a part of the body. And if the ear says, "Because I am not an eye, I am not a part of the body," it is not for this reason any the less a part of the body. If the whole body were an eye, where would the hearing be? If the whole were hearing, where would the sense of smell be? But now God has placed the members, each one of them, in the body, just as He desired. If they were all one member, where would the body be? But now there are many members, but one body. And the eye cannot say to the hand, "I have no need of you"; or again the head to the feet, "I have no need of you." On the contrary, it is much truer that the members of the body which seem to be weaker are necessary; and those members of the body which we deem less honorable, on these we bestow more abundant honor, and our less presentable members become much more presentable, whereas our more presentable members have no need of it. But God has so composed the body, giving more abundant honor to that member which lacked, so that there may be no division in the body, but that the members may have the same care for one another. And if one member suffers, all the members suffer with it; if one member is honored, all the members rejoice with it.

Now you are Christ's body, and individually members of it. And God has appointed in the church, first apostles, second prophets, third teachers, then miracles, then gifts of healings, helps, administrations, various kinds of tongues. All are not apostles, are they? All are not prophets, are they? All are not teachers, are they? All are not workers of miracles, are they? All do not have gifts of healings, do they? All do not speak with tongues, do they? All do not interpret, do they? But earnestly desire the greater gifts.

I show you a still more excellent way.

—1 Cor. 12:12–31

3. It's a Building

For we are His workmanship, created in Christ Jesus for good works, which God prepared beforehand so that we would walk in them.

Therefore remember that formerly you, the Gentiles in the flesh, who are called "Uncircumcision" by the so-called "Circumcision," which is performed in the flesh by human hands—remember *that you were at that time separate from Christ, excluded from the commonwealth of Israel, and strangers to the covenants of promise, having no hope and without God in the world. But now in Christ Jesus you who formerly were far off have been brought near by the blood of Christ. For He Himself is our peace, who made both* groups into *one and broke down the barrier of the dividing wall, by abolishing in His flesh the enmity,* which is *the Law of commandments* contained in *ordinances, so that in Himself He might make the two into one new man,* thus *establishing peace, and might reconcile them both in one body to God through the cross, by it having put to death the enmity.* AND HE CAME AND PREACHED PEACE TO YOU WHO WERE FAR AWAY, AND PEACE TO THOSE WHO WERE NEAR; *for through Him we both have our access in one Spirit to the Father. So then you are no longer strangers and aliens, but you are fellow citizens with the saints, and are of God's household, having been built on the foundation of the apostles and prophets, Christ Jesus Himself being the corner* stone, *in whom the whole building, being fitted together, is growing into a holy temple in the* LORD, *in whom you also are being built together into a dwelling of God in the Spirit.*

—Eph. 2:10–22

4. It's a Bride

For I am jealous for you with a godly jealousy; for I betrothed you to one husband, so that to Christ I might present you as *a pure virgin.*
—2 Cor. 11:2

Prayer: Part 1

Prayer is as old as humankind, as universal as religion, and as instinctive as breathing. People have been praying since the days of Seth: *"To Seth, to him also a son was born; and he called his name Enosh. Then men began to call upon the name of the* Lord*"* (Gen. 4:26, emphasis added). It is practiced in some form by all people of all faiths. Prayer springs from a heart of need. For the Christian, we know there is only one true God, our Creator Jehovah Lord God Almighty. We are told, *"For there is one God, and one mediator also between God and men, the man Christ Jesus"* (1 Tim. 2:5). Jesus said, *"Whatever you ask in My name, that will I do, so that the Father may be glorified in the Son"* (John 14:13).

There are two kinds of prayer: prayers that do not reach God and prayers that do. This fact is illustrated by our Lord in the parable of the Pharisee and the publican:

> *Two men went up into the temple to pray, one a Pharisee and the other a tax collector. The Pharisee stood and was praying this to himself: "God, I thank You that I am not like other people: swindlers, unjust, adulterers, or even like this tax collector. I fast twice a week; I pay tithes of all that I get." But the tax collector, standing some distance away, was even unwilling to lift up his eyes to heaven, but was beating his breast, saying, "God, be merciful to me, the sinner!" I tell you, this man went to his house justified rather than the other; for everyone who exalts himself will be humbled, but he who humbles himself will be exalted.*
>
> —Luke 18:10–14

Both men went to the same place, at the same time, for the same purpose: to pray. The Pharisee prayed in his religious pride, expecting God to answer because he thought himself worthy. He informed God of his own goodness, that he was better than others. He boasted of his good works. He said that he fasted and paid. That is the kind of prayer that does not reach God. It is a self-righteous prayer.

Now look at the publican and his prayer. He came to God in humility, conscious of his unworthiness, confessing himself a sinner, and begging for mercy. This is the kind of prayer that does reach God. This is a righteous prayer.

It is a privilege to pray, because it brings you into close fellowship with God, admitting your need for Him and your utter dependence upon Him.

Now that you know what prayers reach God, let's look at some aspects of prayer.

1. What Is Prayer?

Ask, and it will be given to you; seek, and you will find; knock, and it will be opened to you. For everyone who asks receives, and he who seeks finds, and to him who knocks it will be opened. Or what man is there among you who, when his son asks for a loaf, will give him a stone? Or if he asks for a fish, he will not give him a snake, will he? If you then, being evil, know how to give good gifts to your children, how much more will your Father who is in heaven give what is good to those who ask Him!

—Matt. 7:7–11

2. Why Pray?

Now He was telling them a parable to show that at all times they ought to pray and not to lose heart.

—Luke 18:1

3. How to Pray

Pray, then, in this way:

"Our Father who is in heaven,
Hallowed be Your name.
Your kingdom come.
Your will be done,
On earth as it is in heaven.
Give us this day our daily bread.
And forgive us our debts, as we also have forgiven our debtors.
And do not lead us into temptation, but deliver us from evil.
[For Yours is the kingdom and the power and the glory forever.
Amen."]

—Matt. 6:9–13

4. Where to Pray

Peter was kept in prison, but the church was praying fervently for him (John 3:3–8). In the previous chapter on the church, we discovered that God's church is not a building or denomination. Only blood-washed, born-again, Spirit-baptized believers constitute the church that Jesus is building.

5. Hindrances to Prayer

You husbands in the same way, live with your wives in an understanding way, as with someone weaker, since she is a woman; and show her honor as a fellow heir of the grace of life, so that your prayers will not be hindered.

To sum up, all of you be harmonious, sympathetic, brotherly, kindhearted, and humble in spirit; not returning evil for evil or insult for insult, but giving a blessing instead; for you were called for the very purpose that you might inherit a blessing.

—1 Pet. 3:7–9 emphasis added

6. Does God Answer All Prayers?

If you abide in Me, and My words abide in you, ask whatever you wish, and it shall be done for you. . . . so that whatever you ask of the Father in My name, He may give to you.

—John 15:7, 16

There are different kinds of prayer. Read Matthew 6:6; Acts 10:2, 30; Matthew 18:20; 1 Corinthians 14:14–17; Matthew 21:22; John 14:13; 1 John 5:14; and 1 Thessalonians 5:17.

Sometimes, we find ourselves without words to pray. Often, surrounding negatives—disappointments, anger, separation, hurt feelings—leave us speechless. None of these are of God. We must remember where to go when the negatives creep in and leave us without words; we need to go to Him who understands and gives wisdom and healing, so we can present ourselves worthy of Him to others.

Resist the urge to complicate prayer, remembering God knows your heart. Don't take pride in well-crafted prayers. Don't apologize for incoherent prayers. No games. No cover-ups. Just be honest with yourself and God. Climb into His lap and tell Him everything that's on your mind. Or say nothing at all. Just lift your heart to heaven and declare, "Father." That's enough for your heavenly Father to wrap you in His arms. He knows the secrets of your heart (Ps. 44:21). He will cover you with His feathers to give you refuge; His faithfulness is your protection (Ps. 91:4).

I implore you to seek the Lord and study His Word, the Bible. Pray humbly with love in your heart and always in the name of Jesus.

Faith

The righteous shall live by faith. This declaration of the Christian's principle of life is found four times in the Bible:

> *I will stand on my guard post*
> *And station myself on the rampart;*
> *And I will keep watch to see what He will speak to me,*
> *And how I may reply when I am reproved.*
> *Then the* LORD *answered me and said,*
> *"Record the vision*
> *And inscribe it on tablets,*
> *That the one who reads it may run.*
> *For the vision is yet for the appointed time;*
> *It hastens toward the goal and it will not fail.*
> *Though it tarries, wait for it;*
> *For it will certainly come, it will not delay.*
>
> *"Behold, as for the proud one,*
> *His soul is not right within him;*
> *But the righteous will live by his faith.*
> *Furthermore, wine betrays the haughty man,*
> *So that he does not stay at home.*
> *He enlarges his appetite like Sheol,*
> *And he is like death, never satisfied.*
> *He also gathers to himself all nations*
> *And collects to himself all peoples."*
>
> —Hab. 2:1–5

For in it the righteousness of God is revealed from faith to faith; as it is written, "BUT THE RIGHTEOUS MAN SHALL LIVE BY FAITH."
—Rom. 1:17

For as many as are of the works of the Law are under a curse; for it is written, "CURSED IS EVERYONE WHO DOES NOT ABIDE BY ALL THINGS WRITTEN IN THE BOOK OF THE LAW, TO PERFORM THEM." Now that no one is justified by the Law before God is evident; for, "THE RIGHTEOUS MAN SHALL LIVE BY FAITH."
—Gal. 3:10–11

BUT MY RIGHTEOUS ONE SHALL LIVE BY FAITH;
AND IF HE SHRINKS BACK, MY SOUL HAS NO PLEASURE IN HIM.
—Heb. 10:38

In Habakkuk, we see the difference between the lives of the righteous and the unrighteous. The unrighteous are puffed up and live in their own self-sufficiency. But the righteous live by faith; their confidence is in God. To them, faith is more than a philosophy of life; it is the very principle of life (Hab. 2:4). The righteous shall live their whole lives by faith:

- They are saved by faith: *"Believe in the Lord Jesus, and you will be saved, you and your household"* (Acts 16:31).
- They are kept by faith: *"Who are protected by the power of God through faith for a salvation ready to be revealed in the last time"* (1 Pet. 1:5).
- They live by faith: *"I have been crucified with Christ; and it is no longer I who live, but Christ lives in me; and the life which I now live in the flesh I live by faith in the Son of God, who loved me and gave Himself up for me"* (Gal. 2:20).
- His faith shall be tried many times and in many ways: *"So that the proof of your faith, being more precious than gold which is perishable, even though tested by fire, may be found to result in praise and glory and honor at the revelation of Jesus Christ"* (1 Pet. 1:7).
- Faith will always be vindicated. It knows how to wait for the Lord: *"Yet those who wait for the Lord / Will gain new*

strength; / They will mount up with wings like eagles, / They will run and not get tired, / They will walk and not become weary" (Isa. 40:31).
- Faith is always victorious: *"For whatever is born of God overcomes the world; and this is the victory that has overcome the world—our faith"* (1 John 5:4).
- Faith defies reason; it moves mountains.

When they came to the crowd, a man came up to Jesus, falling on his knees before Him and saying, "Lord, have mercy on my son, for he is a lunatic and is very ill; for he often falls into the fire and often into the water. I brought him to Your disciples, and they could not cure him." And Jesus answered and said, "You unbelieving and perverted generation, how long shall I be with you? How long shall I put up with you? Bring him here to Me." And Jesus rebuked him, and the demon came out of him, and the boy was cured at once.

Then the disciples came to Jesus privately and said, "Why could we not drive it out?" And He said to them, "Because of the littleness of your faith; for truly I say to you, if you have faith the size of a mustard seed, you will say to this mountain, 'Move from here to there,' and it will move; and nothing will be impossible to you. [But this kind does not go out except by prayer and fasting.]"

—Matt. 17:14–21

- Faith does not always face facts; it never gives up.

And what more shall I say? For time will fail me if I tell of Gideon, Barak, Samson, Jephthah, of David and Samuel and the prophets, who by faith conquered kingdoms, performed acts of righteousness, obtained promises, shut the mouths of lions, quenched the power of fire, escaped the edge of the sword, from weakness were made strong, became mighty in war, put foreign armies to flight. Women received back their dead by resurrection; and others were tortured, not accepting their release, so that they might obtain a better resurrection; and others experienced mockings and scourgings, yes, also chains and imprisonment. They were stoned, they were sawn in two, they were tempted, they were put to death with the sword; they went about in sheepskins, in goatskins, being destitute, afflicted, ill-treated (men of whom the world was not worthy), wandering in deserts and mountains and caves and holes in the ground.

And all these, having gained approval through their faith, did not receive what was promised, because God had provided something better for us, so that apart from us they should not be made perfect.
—Heb. 11:32–40

Faith says that God is working out His perfect will in my life, and I can wait, endure, and suffer. Faith does not make anything easy, but it does make all things possible. Let's look at some aspects of faith.

- What Faith Is

Now faith is the assurance of things hoped for, the conviction of things not seen. For by it the men of old gained approval.

By faith we understand that the worlds were prepared by the word of God, so that what is seen was not made out of things which are visible.
—Heb. 11:1–3

- The Importance of Faith

In addition to all, taking up the shield of faith with which you will be able to extinguish all the flaming arrows of the evil one.
—Eph. 6:16

- Little Faith

Peter said to Him, "Lord, if it is You, command me to come to You on the water." And He said, "Come!" And Peter got out of the boat, and walked on the water and came toward Jesus. But seeing the wind, he became frightened, and beginning to sink, he cried out, "Lord, save me!" Immediately Jesus stretched out His hand and took hold of him, and said to him, "You of little faith, why did you doubt?" When they got into the boat, the wind stopped. And those who were in the boat worshiped Him, saying, "You are certainly God's Son!"
—Matt. 14:28–33

Faith

- Three Kinds of Faith
  1. Limited faith: Martha believed Jesus had to be there to heal Lazarus.
  2. Fundamental faith: Martha believed Lazarus would rise again in the resurrection as taught.
  3. Unlimited faith: Martha consented to remove the stone. She believed in the power in Jesus to raise the dead on earth.

Martha then said to Jesus, "Lord, if You had been here, my brother would not have died. Even now I know that whatever You ask of God, God will give You." Jesus said to her, "Your brother will rise again." Martha said to Him, "I know that he will rise again in the resurrection on the last day." Jesus said to her, "I am the resurrection and the life; he who believes in Me will live even if he dies, and everyone who lives and believes in Me will never die. Do you believe this?" She said to Him, "Yes, Lord; I have believed that You are the Christ, the Son of God, even *He who comes into the world."*

When she had said this, she went away and called Mary her sister, saying secretly, "The Teacher is here and is calling for you." And when she heard it, she got up quickly and was coming to Him.

Now Jesus had not yet come into the village, but was still in the place where Martha met Him. Then the Jews who were with her in the house, and consoling her, when they saw that Mary got up quickly and went out, they followed her, supposing that she was going to the tomb to weep there. Therefore, when Mary came where Jesus was, she saw Him, and fell at His feet, saying to Him, "Lord, if You had been here, my brother would not have died." When Jesus therefore saw her weeping, and the Jews who came with her also *weeping, He was deeply moved in spirit and was troubled, and said, "Where have you laid him?" They said to Him, "Lord, come and see." Jesus wept. So the Jews were saying, "See how He loved him!" But some of them said, "Could not this man, who opened the eyes of the blind man, have kept this man also from dying?"*

So Jesus, again being deeply moved within, came to the tomb. Now it was a cave, and a stone was lying against it. Jesus said, "Remove the stone." Martha, the sister of the deceased, said to Him, "Lord, by this time there will be a stench, for he has been dead four days." Jesus said to her, "Did I not say to you that if you believe, you will see the glory of God?" So they removed the stone. Then Jesus raised His eyes, and said, "Father, I thank You that You have heard Me. I knew that You always hear Me; but because of the people standing around I said it, so that they may believe that You sent Me." When He had said these things, He cried out with a loud voice, "Lazarus, come forth." The man who had died came forth, bound hand and foot with wrappings, and his face was wrapped around with a cloth. Jesus said to them, "Unbind him, and let him go."

—John 11:21–44

Strengthen your faith today with remembrances from the hall of faith.

And what more shall I say? For time will fail me if I tell of Gideon, Barak, Samson, Jephthah, of David and Samuel and the prophets, who by faith conquered kingdoms, performed acts of righteousness, obtained promises, shut the mouths of lions, quenched the power of fire, escaped the edge of the sword, from weakness were made strong, became mighty in war, put foreign armies to flight. Women received back their dead by resurrection; and others were tortured, not accepting their release, so that they might obtain a better resurrection; and others experienced mockings and scourgings, yes, also chains and imprisonment. They were stoned, they were sawn in two, they were tempted, they were put to death with the sword; they went about in sheepskins, in goatskins, being destitute, afflicted, ill-treated (men of whom the world was not worthy), wandering in deserts and mountains and caves and holes in the ground.

And all these, having gained approval through their faith, did not receive what was promised, because God had provided something better for us, so that apart from us they would not be made perfect.

—Heb. 11:32–40

He limitlessly increases your faith as you trust Him in and through all things.

3. The abundant life is a separated life.

Paul, a bond-servant of Christ Jesus, called as an apostle, set apart for the gospel of God.

—Rom. 1:1

4. The abundant life is a Spirit-filled life.

And do not get drunk with wine, for that is dissipation, but be filled with the Spirit, speaking to one another in psalms and hymns and spiritual songs, singing and making melody with your heart to the Lord; always giving thanks for all things in the name of our Lord Jesus Christ to God, even the Father; and be subject to one another in the fear of Christ.

—Eph. 5:18–20

5. The abundant life is a mature life.

But grow in the grace and knowledge of our Lord and Savior Jesus Christ. To Him be the glory, both now and to the day of eternity. Amen.

—2 Pet. 3:18

All Scripture is inspired by God and profitable for teaching, for reproof, for correction, for training in righteousness; so that the man of God may be adequate, equipped for every good work.

—2 Tim. 3:16–17

Repentance

Repentance is turning away from sin with the renewing of one's mind, becoming one with God. Consider Proverbs 28:13: *"He who conceals his transgressions will not prosper. But he who confesses and forsakes* them *will find compassion."* God desires *"truth in the innermost being"* (Ps. 51:6) and commands all people everywhere to repent (Acts 17:30). Sinners must repent before they can receive salvation by grace through faith (Eph. 2:8–9). The saved must practice repentance if they are to enjoy unbroken fellowship with God (Job 42:1–6).

Repentance is granted by God (Acts 5:31, 11:18). Paul said, *"The kindness of God leads you to repentance"* (Rom. 2:4).

The kindness of God is not merited; it is a gift that results in repentance. This gift of repentance is an inward change produced by the convicting power of the Holy Spirit as we hear the Word of God (Acts 2:37–38, John 16:7–11).

Repentance qualifies a person for salvation, but it takes faith in Christ to acquire it. True repentance is always coupled with faith. Without repentance, faith is the ultimate hypocrisy. Repentance without faith in the death, burial, and resurrection of Christ is folly.

Let's look at some aspects of repentance:

1. Defined

The Lord is not slow about His promise, as some count slowness, but is patient toward you, not wishing for any to perish but for all to come to repentance.

—2 Pet. 3:9

Repentance

2. Preached

The beginning of the gospel of Jesus Christ, the Son of God. As it is written in Isaiah the prophet:

> *"Behold, I send My messenger ahead of You,*
> *Who will prepare Your way;*
> *The voice of one crying in the wilderness,*
> *'Make ready the way of the Lord,*
> *Make His paths straight.'"*

John the Baptist appeared in the wilderness preaching a baptism of repentance for the forgiveness of sins.

—Mark 1:1–4

3. Free from Dead Works

Therefore leaving the elementary teaching about the Christ, let us press on to maturity, not laying again a foundation of repentance from dead works and of faith toward God.

—Heb. 6:1

4. God's Role

For they indeed became priests without an oath, but He with an oath through the One who said to Him,

> *"The Lord has sworn*
> *And will not change His mind,*
> *'You are a priest forever.'"*

—Heb. 7:21

5. Impossible to Renew

For in the case of those who have once been enlightened and have tasted of the heavenly gift and have been made partakers of the Holy Spirit, and have tasted the good word of God and the powers of the age to come, and then *have fallen away, it is impossible to renew them again to repentance, since they again crucify to themselves the Son of God, and put Him to open shame.*

—Heb. 6:4–6

6. Importance

Therefore having overlooked the times of ignorance, God is now declaring to men that all people everywhere should repent, because He has fixed a day in which He will judge the world in righteousness through a Man whom He has appointed, having furnished proof to all men by raising Him from the dead.

—Acts 17:30–31

7. Evidence

So, King Agrippa, I did not prove disobedient to the heavenly vision, but kept declaring both to those of Damascus first, and also at Jerusalem and then throughout all the region of Judea, and even to the Gentiles, that they should repent and turn to God, performing deeds appropriate to repentance.

—Acts 26:19–20

We are sinners; therefore, we must daily repent and renew our minds to the Word of God, become one with Him, and spread the good news of our risen Lord and Savior Jesus Christ Who died for our sins. The Bible is the greatest instructional book for daily life that has ever been written. Because God cannot lie (Heb. 6:18, Titus 1:2), we can find encouragement and hope. His Word is perfect, and we can be perfected through it. Seek Him diligently. Lean not on your own understanding but upon Him and His Word. Ask His Holy Spirit to give you wisdom as you seek Him.

The New Birth

It's important to understand what Jesus meant when He told Nicodemus, *"Truly, truly, I say to you, unless one is born again he cannot see the kingdom of God"* (John 3:3). This new birth is a spiritual birth. It's as much a birth as the natural birth, not just a figure of speech. The first birth is of the seed of man. The second birth is of the seed of God, *"not of seed which is perishable but imperishable, that is, through the living and enduring Word of God"* (1 Pet. 1:23).

What is the new birth?

- It is a new creation (2 Cor. 5:17).
- It is a spiritual resurrection (Eph. 2:1–9).
- It is a regeneration (Titus 3:5).
- It is partaking of the divine nature of God (2 Pet. 1:4).
- It is receiving Jesus Christ as Savior and Lord by faith (John 1:12).
- It is being made the *"righteousness of God"* (2 Cor. 5:21).
- It is necessary to become a child of God: *"You* must *be born again"* (John 3:7, emphasis added).

1. Jesus and the Two Births

Now there was a man of the Pharisees, named Nicodemus, a ruler of the Jews; this man came to Jesus by night and said to Him, "Rabbi, we know that You have come from God as a teacher; for no one can do these signs that You do unless God is with him." Jesus answered and said to him, "Truly, truly, I say to you, unless one is born again he cannot see the kingdom of God."

Nicodemus said to Him, "How can a man be born when he is old? He cannot enter a second time into his mother's womb and be born, can he?" Jesus answered, "Truly, truly, I say to you, unless one is born of water and the Spirit he cannot enter into the kingdom of God. That which is born of the flesh is flesh, and that which is born of the Spirit is spirit. Do not be amazed that I said to you, 'You must be born again.' The wind blows where it wishes and you hear the sound of it, but do not know where it comes from and where it is going; so is everyone who is born of the Spirit."

—John 3:1–8

2. A New, Sinless Nature

No one who is born of God practices sin, because His seed abides in him; and he cannot sin, because he is born of God.

—1 John 3:9

3. Imperishable

For you have been born again not of seed which is perishable but imperishable, that is, *through the living and abiding word of God.*

—1 Pet. 1:23

4. The Means

As Moses lifted up the serpent in the wilderness, even so must the Son of Man be lifted up; so that whoever believes will in Him have eternal life.

   For God so loved the world, that He gave his only begotten Son, that whoever believes in Him shall not perish, but have eternal life. For God did not send the Son into the world to judge the world, but that the world might be saved through Him. He who believes in Him is not judged; he who does not believe has been judged already, because he has not believed in the name of the only begotten Son of God.

—John 3:14–18

5. Victory

Whoever believes that Jesus is the Christ is born of God, and whoever loves the Father loves the child *born of Him. By this we know that we love the children of God, when we love God and observe His*

commandments. For this is the love of God, that we keep His commandments; and His commandments are not burdensome.
—1 John 5:1–3

Through Him, we are born again, saved, victorious—able to live eternally with God Almighty.

Paul's Farewell to Ephesus

In his farewell to Ephesus, Paul's directives reflect the church of today.

> *With all humility and many tears I did my work as the Lord's servant during the hard times that came to me because of the plots of some Jews. You know that I did not hold back anything that would be of help to you as I preached and taught in public and in your homes. To Jews and Gentiles alike I gave solemn warning that they should turn from their sins to God and believe in our Lord Jesus. For I have not held back from announcing to you the whole purpose of God. So keep watch over yourselves and over all the flock which the Holy Spirit has placed in your care. Be shepherds of the church of God, which he made his own through the blood of his Son.*
> —Acts 20:19–21, 27–28 GNT

In verse 19, Paul did his work with all humility and many tears. Why tears? They were tears of hard times and suffering, of grief for those who did not believe. God does not promise that we will have a smooth journey as we spread His Word. In fact, Jesus said *"And he who does not take his cross and follow after Me is not worthy of Me"* (Matt. 10:38).

How did Jesus live His life? Read Matthew, Mark, Luke, and John and pray for the Holy Spirit to give you wisdom. Here are some key takeaways:

1. Become like Jesus.

Matthew 10:24–25 has one of the first great principles of discipleship: become like the Master. Paul echoed this principle in

Galatians 4:19: *"My children, with whom I am again in labor until Christ is formed in you."*

2. Practice the triumph of a faithful disciple.

Contrary to popular belief, becoming a Christian doesn't eradicate all trials, problems, and difficulties from life. The adage that God will not give us more than we can bear is *not* in the Bible. Instead, He tells us, *"No temptation has overtaken you but such as is common to man; and God is faithful, who will not allow you to be tempted beyond what you are able, but with the temptation will provide the way of escape also, so that you may be able to endure it"* (1 Cor. 10:13).

Indeed, Jesus warns the disciples that the Christian life will be like His own life was. If the world crucified Christ, what will it do to the servant of Christ? If the world accused Jesus of working through satan's power, what will it say about us? Surely no less evil. Despite these dire predictions, Jesus says that God is watching and caring. No matter what happens, always stand for truth, because God is with you.

After warning His disciples of the trials to come, Jesus encourages them, saying, *"Therefore everyone who confesses Me before men, I will also confess him before My Father who is in heaven"* (Matt. 10:32). No matter what the world does to you, stand for Jesus and His Word, and when judgment day comes, Jesus will stand with you before God. What a wonderful encouragement to stay faithful. No matter what the world does to His disciples, Jesus will not forsake you. In the final reckoning, Jesus will stand with you before God and say, "This one has been faithful and is mine." That will be the disciple's ultimate triumph.

3. Heed the warning to unfaithful disciples.

Jesus defends faithful disciples, but He warns the disciple who diverts from service in the pressures and threats of the world. Jesus tells His disciples, *"But whoever denies Me before men, I will also deny him before My Father who is in heaven"* (Matt. 10:33). Where the faithful will experience the ultimate triumph, the unfaithful will experience the ultimate rejection—denied by Jesus.

Perhaps the greatest challenge to faithfulness comes not from strangers but from loved ones. Family objection has caused many to turn from the faith. Jesus says very clearly that He must come first. No matter how close or dear family members may be, they must not be allowed to come between disciples and their Lord.

4. Take up the cross.

In Matthew 10:38, Jesus says, *"And he who does not take his cross and follow after Me is not worthy of Me."* Today, the expression "take up your cross" has been so trivialized that few really know its meaning. We hear someone say of chronic illness, "That is just the cross I have to bear." Others joke about a spouse: "He's my cross in life." In other words, anything perceived as unpleasant or hard is the cross one is expected to bear. This is not the way Jesus meant the phrase.

To take your cross is literally to relinquish your life. Imagine standing on a first-century street corner and talking to a friend when you hear commotion down the street. You turn and see a squad of Roman soldiers coming toward you, leading a man struggling with a cross. That is a common sight; you have seen it before. You know what's about to happen. Soon the man will be outside the city gates and nailed to the very cross he was carrying, where he will hang until he is dead.

This is the picture Jesus conveyed when He said, "Take up your cross." He wasn't asking for a general commitment but rather total commitment. Jesus wants your life. Just as the man carrying the cross must give up his life to the Romans, so must Christ's disciples give up their lives to Him. Jesus determines how each surrendered life will be lived.

5. It is a wonderful paradox.

In order to hear Jesus, you must confess Him before God and relinquish your life to Him. So Jesus concludes, *"He who has found his life shall lose it, and he who has lost his life for My sake will find it"* (Matt. 10:39).

Do we take our cross and follow Him daily in all walks and situations? Are we examples before everyone? Do we allow the sins of others to bring out the worst in us, or do we rebuke the sin and love the person? Do we walk away calmly as Christ exemplified? Do we let others know of the salvation they have through Jesus Christ and His shed blood on the cross? Do we speak to those who need salvation, or do we play it safe and stand with believers, speaking His Word among the already saved? Jesus walked among the unsaved, teaching them to be born again. Do we beg forgiveness and renew our minds when we sin? Do we even know every moment we sin? God does. He will help us when we allow Him to.

Reflect on the cross, Christ's walk to Golgotha, His scourging, the nails in His body. Consider what that means for us today: eternal life because Christ arose and ascended to the right hand of God Almighty. He was not confined to the grave. He lives!

For further reading, see Matthew 26:26–28, 27:28–66, and 28:1–20.

Creation

Colossians 1:16–17 states:
For by Him all things were created, both in the heavens and on earth, visible and invisible, whether thrones or dominions or rulers or authorities—all things have been created through Him and for Him. He is before all things, and in Him all things hold together.

God created all things, visible and invisible. And *"God created man in His own image"* (Gen. 1:27).

God's plan from the beginning was salvation through the cross. We were created by Him and for Him. His Word spoke us into being, and His Word became Jesus Christ who died on the cross for our salvation, our eternal life.

Why do you think we were created by Him and for Him?

He created us for His delight, to watch us enjoy His creation, do our best in life, grow in Him, and share that with others. He wants us to help others and care for His creation, to appreciate all He's given to us. He wants us to hold fast to the cross, Jesus Christ, His Word, and the Holy Spirit. He wants to fill us with His Spirit and love. Rejoice, for each day is a day He has made.

Let us rejoice and exult
   and give him the glory,
for the marriage of the Lamb has come,
   and his Bride [God's church] has made herself ready.
—Rev. 19:7 ESV

Creation

Jehovah Jireh provides for us. Jehovah Shammah is always there. Jehovah Nissi gives us victory, and through Jehovah Rapha we are healed. God must have given great thought to His creation.

Transformation

Do not be conformed to this world, but be transformed by the renewal of your mind, that by testing you may discern what is the will of God, what is good and acceptable and perfect.

—Rom. 12:2 ESV

Therefore if anyone is in Christ, he is a new creation. The old has passed away; behold, the new has come.

—2 Cor. 5:17 ESV

The changes that have seemed long in coming will now take place in rapid succession. Be flexible. I will carry you through the things that are beyond your ability to control. Go with the flow, says the Lord. There is no need to worry or to be afraid because I am with you to speak to your heart and to give you direction. Yours is only to surrender in obedience.

—Marsha Burns

*If they hear and serve Him,
They will end their days in prosperity
And their years in pleasures.*

—Job 36:11

*You will make known to me the path of life;
In Your presence is fullness of joy;
In Your right hand there are pleasures forever.*

—Ps. 16:11

Transformation

As we walk the path God designed for us, we see that Jesus Christ is the only way to reach the end of that path. He leads to the light—eternal life in His presence. That path is one-directional; it doesn't have double lanes for passing. God's law and instruction are designed to make us stronger, healthier, able to live a better life and walk a straight path to Him, staying in His presence, living the abundant life that Christ came to give.

Having a new mind is a step-by-step process that requires growing in Christ both individually and as the church of Christ. Each member does his or her part, building each other up in love (Eph. 4:15–16). Growing as a church involves discerning the body of Christ, not knowing each other spiritually (2 Cor. 5:16). It involves continually submitting to the Holy Spirit and allowing God's grace to work through us in thought, word, and deed. It involves doing the God-generated works of repentance (Matt. 3:8). It involves Godly sorrow (2 Cor. 7:9–11). All these things work together to transfigure us from glory to glory.

God's intent is that you change your mind or, literally, have a new mind. The original language carries the nuances of compassion and sorrow. For example, *metanoeo* and *metamellomai* mean to have a new mind, while other words mean to be sorry. Remember, the English word *repent* means to turn around and proceed in the opposite direction. It may be that the translators themselves didn't quite understand the clear distinction between what God requires of us (to have a new mind) and the human emotion of sorrow, although sorrow is obviously part of repentance. Repentance is an unfolding revelation, a new mind, and through it, God will continue to remove the veil and give us a better understanding of scripture.

> *Therefore I urge you, brethren, by the mercies of God, to present your bodies a living and holy sacrifice, acceptable to God, which is your spiritual service of worship. And do not be conformed to this world, but be transformed by the renewing of your mind, so that you*

> *may prove what the will of God is, that which is good and acceptable and perfect.*
>
> —Rom. 12:1–2

Transformed comes from the Greek word *metamorphoo*. From it, we get the English word *metamorphosis*. Metamorphosis is a change from one thing into another.

The mind battles. The enemy of our souls creates in us a self-serving, opinionated self that ultimately separates us from the ones we love and uses every trick to keep our minds captive to him. He does that by lying, but the truth sets us free. The Holy Spirit, our Helper, guides us into all truth and strengthens our faith. Faith comes by hearing and hearing by the Word of God (Rom. 10:17). As we grow in love for our Savior and His Word, transforming into a Christ-like image, the evil in our hearts dies, and our hearts are cleansed of the filth and lies. *"If we confess our sins, He is faithful and righteous to forgive our sins and to cleanse us from all unrighteousness"* (1 John 1:9).

Satan will try to direct your mind. He will bring to your mind past sins you have laid at the cross. When he does, bring up the works suitable for repentance. There should be sorrow over and hatred of sin. There should be humility but not self-condemnation.

Every sin has victims and limits your ministry to others. Those sins are covered by the blood. Don't allow the memories of them to stir up regrets, allowing condemnation to set in, which comes from the evil one. He may do that secretly in your own mind or publicly through other people or members of the church. *"Submit therefore to God. Resist the devil and he will flee from you"* (James 4:7).

> *Brethren, even if anyone is caught in any trespass, you who are spiritual, restore such a one in a spirit of gentleness; each one looking to yourself, so that you too will not be tempted. Bear one another's burdens, and thereby fulfill the law of Christ. For if anyone thinks he is something when he is nothing, he deceives himself. But each one*

Walk in the Light

We must act like His children—because we are. As we grow, we mature: we seek Him, His Word, and His wisdom. Like children, we run to Him when we are in trouble. Likewise, we should seek Him in all things as our children seek us.

When children receive gifts, they gleam with joy and show the gifts to their friends and relatives. Children are loved, cared for, and disciplined for their betterment and protection. We should respond as children when we accept our Father in heaven and trust in Him, for He is the greatest Father of all. Through Jehovah Tsidkenu (God our Righteousness), we have righteousness (1 Cor. 1:30) because of Jesus Christ.

Learning to rely totally on Him for everything is hard for adults, but we must because He can and will care for us. We must walk in harmony with Him down our daily paths. What I thought were dark moments in my past were revealed later as the light of Christ shining on me, taking me through the path He designed for me. He never promised us a rose garden, but He did promise to be with us always—He is Jehovah Raah, the Good Shepherd. He tends to His flock without ceasing. He is Jehovah Nissi, our victory. *"Offer the sacrifices of righteousness, and trust in the Lord"* (Ps. 4:5).

Remember this: trust and rely on Him. Live a better life. Be good to others, for He places people in our paths to help us and test us. He does not lead us to temptation but to Christ-likeness. We are to offer kindness and words of inspiration and wisdom, guided by the Holy Spirit. Pray for discernment, not leaning upon your own understanding, not fearing or dreading or seeking revenge. Jesus is our example. Walk in His light through the darkest and brightest moments of life with confidence. Smile and be full of joy, for He knows the path He designed for us, one that leads directly to Him now and forevermore.

Daily Testing

A gentle answer turns away wrath,
But a harsh word stirs up anger.
The tongue of the wise makes knowledge acceptable,
But the mouth of fools spouts folly.
The eyes of the LORD are in every place,
Watching the evil and the good.
A soothing tongue is a tree of life,
But perversion in it crushes the spirit.

—Prov. 15:1–4

Test yourselves to see if you are in the faith; examine yourselves! Or do you not recognize this about yourselves, that Jesus Christ is in you—unless indeed you fail the test?

—2 Cor. 13:5

I question myself daily. The closer the walk we take with our Lord Jesus Christ, the more the adversary wants to tear that walk apart and lead us down another path—his path (John 10:10). His path is one of doubt, confusion, and negative thoughts and words. He preys on our weaknesses and the weaknesses of others, examining our faults and blinding us from seeing the good. It's the walk of death. Sometimes, my smile disappears, and my weaknesses surface. I question if I am doing all I can do to please my heavenly Father. Then I snap out of it and rebuke the adversary. I pray, seek God, and get in the Word, inviting the Holy Spirit to give me light and wisdom. I repent and accept forgiveness, remembering that Jesus came to give us life abundantly.

I want to reflect His gentleness and knowledge, to speak His soothing words that produce life. Through Him is our righteousness. We must look for the good, lift up the good in ourselves and others, and speak goodness over one another until it crowds out the weaknesses, the negatives. We are all called to be disciples.

In Matthew 28:19–20, Jesus said to His disciples, *"Go therefore and make disciples of all the nations, baptizing them in the name of the Father, and the Son and the Holy Spirit, teaching them to observe all that I commanded you; and lo, I am with you always, even to the end of the age"* (emphasis added).

In Matthew 10:19–20, Christ said, *"But when they hand you over, do not worry about how or what you are to say; for it will be given you in that hour what you are to say. For it is not you who speak, but it is the Spirit of your Father who speaks in you."*

I so love the song by Matthew West, "Do Something." He sings, "I thought, 'God why won't you do something?'. . . He said, 'I did.' Yeah. 'I created you.'" The song later says, "I wanna be the one who stands up and says, 'I'm gonna do something.'"[1]

Let's all stand up and do something! When we have the opportunity to share and do good and speak kind, uplifting words of our Lord. Do it! We have a responsibility to our loved ones first, to be firm in His discipline and full of love in the Lord, and love all as God loves us, praying earnestly for His wisdom and guidance in all we do.

Let the life of His Spirit spring up in you like a fresh flow of pure water. Let it flood your soul and bring new hope and freedom. It is time for you to completely let go of everything that has kept you bound in darkness. Break out! Rise up! Be filled with the joy of new life.

---

1. Matthew West, "Do Something," *AZLyrics*, https://www.azlyrics.com/lyrics/matthewwest/dosomething.html.

The Church: Its Worship and Work

You are at a point of spiritual discovery. If you will allow it, I will reveal greater depth and meaning in the truth of My Word. However, you will need to yield to the moving of My Spirit and not stubbornly hang on to the traditions of men and the works of the flesh. Open your heart and mind to receive revelation, says the Lord. I am bringing you higher.

—Marsha Burns

But get up and stand on your feet; for this purpose I have appeared to you, to appoint you a minister and a witness not only to the things which you have seen, but also to the things in which I will appear to you.

—Acts 26:16

Go therefore and make disciples of all the nations, baptizing them in the name of the Father and the Son and the Holy Spirit, teaching them to observe all that I commanded you; and lo, I am with you always, even to the end of the age.

—Matt. 28:19–20

When they bring you before the synagogues and the rulers and the authorities, do not worry about how or what you are to speak in your defense, or what you are to say; for the Holy Spirit will teach you in that very hour what you ought to say.

—Luke 12:11–12

The Church: Its Worship and Work

Be dressed in readiness, and keep your lamps lit. You too, be ready; for the Son of Man is coming at an hour that you do not expect.
—Luke 12:35, 40

"For truly in this city there were gathered together against Your holy servant Jesus, whom You anointed, both Herod and Pontius Pilate, along with the Gentiles and the peoples of Israel, to do whatever Your hand and Your purpose predestined to occur. And now, Lord, take note of their threats, and grant that Your bond-servants may speak Your word with all confidence, while You extend Your hand to heal, and signs and wonders take place through the name of Your holy servant Jesus." And when they had prayed, the place where they had gathered together was shaken, and they were all filled with the Holy Spirit and began to speak the word of God with boldness.
—Acts 4:27–31

And my message and my preaching were not in persuasive words of wisdom, but in demonstration of the Spirit and of power, so that your faith would not rest on the wisdom of men, but on the power of God. Now we have received, not the spirit of the world, but the Spirit who is from God, so that we may know the things freely given to us by God, which things we also speak, not in words taught by human wisdom, but in those taught by the Spirit, combining spiritual thoughts with spiritual words.
—1 Cor. 2:4–5, 12–13

*Trust in the Lord with all your heart
And do not lean on your own understanding.
In all your ways acknowledge Him,
And He will make your paths straight.
Do not be wise in your own eyes;
Fear the Lord and turn away from evil.
It will be healing to your body
And refreshment to your bones.*
—Prov. 3:5–8

I urge you to read your Bible just as you would read a book—cover to cover. Seek the Holy Spirit to give you understanding. I personally enjoy reading the New Testament first, maybe because of my upbringing and belief in Christ or because of a New Testament my husband and I kept in our house. I picked it up to read one day while resting with a difficult pregnancy. I believe God had that Bible there for me. I read it four times with the Holy Spirit guiding me and giving me wisdom. I couldn't stop reading. I became so close to Him, and my faith soared during that time. I lost the baby in the fifth month, but I was grateful for the wisdom He had brought me during my days of rest.

When we are too busy for God or caught up in the pleasures of the world, God will bring us to a place where we must be still and hear Him so He can bring us to a better and more fruitful walk with Him. He loves us and will not give up on us. We are here for a purpose, with a choice to hear Him.

After I read the New Testament, I read the Old Testament, seeking God's instruction and wisdom in the Psalms and Proverbs. I still study the Bible as He leads me. To thoroughly understand Revelation, we must understand the Old Testament. We are in the end times, and it is up to us, the church, to spread the gospel for all generations to receive Christ as Savior. Life on earth is temporal, and we are here for His purpose. Life with Him is eternal. *"So faith comes from hearing, and hearing by the Word of God"* (Rom. 10:17, emphasis added).

Make a Difference

There are new possibilities on the horizon. Take this time to prepare yourself by re-evaluating your priorities. I speak to you in terms of spiritual reality and eternal values, which ultimately must take precedence over all things worldly and temporary. Rise up to new heights where you can truly live in the Spirit, says the Lord.

—Marsha Burns

While we look not at the things which are seen, but at the things which are not seen; for the things which are seen are temporal, but the things which are not seen are eternal.

—2 Cor. 4:18

Therefore be imitators of God, as beloved children; and walk in love, just as Christ also loved you and gave Himself up for us, an offering and a sacrifice to God as a fragrant aroma. But immorality or any impurity or greed must not even be named among you, as is proper among saints; and there must be no filthiness and silly talk, or coarse jesting, which are not fitting, but rather giving of thanks.

—Eph. 5:1–4

For you were formerly darkness, but now you are Light in the Lord; walk as children of Light (for the fruit of the Light consists in all goodness and righteousness and truth), trying to learn what is pleasing to the Lord.

—Eph. 5:8–10

Seek the Lord in all that you do and speak, walking in the light of Christ, paying attention to the Holy Spirit as He guides and give you wisdom. Make a difference!

How do Christians stand out to make a positive impression? Perhaps someone drops something, and you quickly move to pick it up. Perhaps someone is sad or has a frown on their face. A smile or a greeting can mean the world to that person. When neighbors need a hand, give them more than they need, and when someone needs prayer, pray right then; do not postpone it. When there are those in need of your experience with Jesus, share. Step up in faith to be the disciple Jesus called you to be. Plant the seeds of faith, allow another to water, and God will cause the seed to grow and flourish. Allow the Holy Spirit to guide you in the direction you need to go, according to God's will. The smile on your face will draw others to you, and you will make a difference.

> *Oh give thanks to the Lord, call upon His name;*
> *Make known His deeds among the peoples.*
> *Sing to Him, sing praises to Him;*
> *Speak of all His wonders.*
> *Glory in His holy name;*
> *Let the heart of those who seek the Lord be glad.*
>
> —Ps. 105:1–3

Healing

Healing can be a spiritual need or a physical need. Be courageous and bold without fear or doubt. Trust Jehovah Rapha who heals and Jehovah Jireh who provides for all your needs, and believe the victory we have through Jehovah Nissi, the victor. Believing for healing is critical. Do not fear, for He is with us, and do not be dismayed, because our God is Almighty. He is our Father, our Creator, and what is impossible for humans is possible through Him. Be refreshed in your mind by His Word, and choose to trust, believe, and have faith in your healing. Fight! Seek a quiet place. Pray and seek His Word to command the enemy to leave. Dress yourself in the armor God provides (Eph. 6:10-18). Write His scripture on your palm for easy view. Do not allow the evil one to steal your joy. Walk with a smile of confidence in your Savior—Jehovah Rapha—who heals.

> *Bless the LORD, O my soul,*
> *And forget none of His benefits;*
> *Who pardons all your iniquities,*
> *Who heals all your diseases;*
> *Who redeems your life from the pit,*
> *Who crowns you with lovingkindness and compassion;*
> *Who satisfies your years with good things,*
> *So that your youth is renewed like the eagle.*
>
> —Ps. 103:2-5

We have power and benefits through the Holy Spirit. He heals *all* our diseases—and the Word does say *all*. Trust Him and be bold in the power of His Word. Know what His Word says and stand on it, relying on His Holy Spirit for guidance. Our body is, after all, a temple for the Holy Spirit to dwell in, so we must strive to take care of our bodies in a manner that is pleasing to Him. Often we rely more on what people say is good rather than trusting God for what is good.

Know and claim His Word for yourself, taking a stand with Jesus as His followers did throughout the Bible. Let His Word live in your heart. Reap His benefits. The Word of God imparts life to us, and that life restores the body with every breath we take and word we speak. We overcome the world, the flesh, and the devil by the blood of the Lamb.

Know the Bible. Live His Word. Speak His Word.

- Jesus was wounded for our transgressions and bruised for our sin. The chastisement for our peace was put on Him on the cross; therefore, we are dead to sin and alive unto the righteousness of God in Christ Jesus, and by *His stripes we are healed* (Isa. 53:5, 1 Pet. 2:24, Rom. 6:11, 2 Cor. 5:21).
- God restores health to our bodies and heals *all* our wounds (Jer. 30:17).
- God has set His love upon us and delivers us. God sets us on high because we know His holy name. We can call on Him, and He will answer. God is with us in times of trouble. He delivers and honors and satisfies us with long life as He continually shows us His salvation (Ps. 91:14–16).
- God sent His Word and healed us. He delivers us from our own destruction. Praise the Lord! (Ps. 107:20).
- The Lord strengthens us in times of illness. He sustains us on our sickbed (Ps. 41:3).
- Obey the Lord when He calls you and asks you to listen to His Word. Don't let His Word depart from your eyes. Keep His Word in your heart because it is life to your spirit and health to your body (Prov. 4:20–22).
- Speak pleasant words because they are like a honeycomb—sweetness to the soul and health to the bones (Prov. 16:24).

Healing

- Like Naaman, do what God, Jehovah, Almighty in heaven says, knowing that obedience is a vital step in being made whole (2 Kings 5:1–15).
- Like Hezekiah, pray and open your heart with tears to Jesus. Walk before God in truth and with a perfect heart, doing what is right in His sight. Use medicine as it is needed, and the Lord will cause you to recover (2 Kings 20:1–11).
- Since Jesus is Lord over your life, forbid sin, sickness, and disease to have any power over you. You are forgiven and free from sin and guilt. We are dead to sin and alive unto the righteousness of God (Col. 1:21–22).
- Release unforgiveness and strife. Choose to forgive others as Christ has forgiven you, for God's love has been shed abroad in our hearts by the Holy Spirit (Matt. 6:12, Eccles. 11:10).
- Heavenly Father, I attend to Your Word; I incline my ears to Your sayings; I refuse to let them depart from my eyes. I keep them in the midst of my heart, for they are life, health, and medicine to all my flesh (Prov. 4:20–22).
- No evil will befall us, neither shall any plague come near our dwelling, for all our places are surrounded by His hedge of protection, for God has given His angels charge over us. They keep us safe in all our ways. In our pathway are life, healing, and health (Ps. 91:10–11, Prov. 12:28).
- The same Spirit that raised Christ Jesus from the dead dwells in us, permeating our veins with resurrection life, sending healing throughout the body (Rom. 8:11).
- *"The thief comes only to steal and kill and destroy; I came that they may have life, and have it abundantly"* (John 10:10).

Thank Jesus for the abundant life in Him. Desire from the heart to live with all His benefits, knowing that His definition of *abundant* differs from what people deem abundant. Claim His Word. Allow Him to speak to your body, telling it to align with His Word. With thanksgiving, create your body a worthy temple for the Holy Spirit, which guides you and reveals His Word with knowledge and discernment. Repent of your sinful self, striving daily for a heart filled with God's unconditional *agape* love that you might draw others to Christ.

Read His scriptures below as a guide to speak your needs before Christ.

- Psalm 107:20
- Ecclesiastes 10:11
- John 6:8
- John 10:28
- 1 John 5:11, 13–15, 20
- Exodus 23:25–26
- Romans 12:1–2
- John 14:20
- 1 Corinthians 6:19
- Matthew 15:13
- Galatians 3:13
- Colossians 1:13–14
- Genesis 1:28–31
- Mark 11:23
- Luke 17:6
- 1 John 5:14–15
- John 6:63
- Mark 11:23
- 1 John 4:4

Personal Changes

God's children struggle between their flesh and their spirit. The flesh is not compatible with the spirit; the flesh longs for what is of the world and feeds its appetite. The Christian's spirit longs for God's righteousness. As we walk through the seasons of our lives, we see the results of our fleshly walk, and we realize there must be more. Our desire to walk in the Light becomes real, and we begin to command the flesh to line up with the Word of God by the authority we are given through the Holy Spirit. Yet the seasons continue to come like waves tossing us to and fro, like a thorn in our side, causing us weakness. We call to our God for help.

And He has said to me, "My grace is sufficient for you, for power is perfected in weakness."

—2 Cor. 12:9

How great is Your goodness,
Which You have stored up for those who fear You,
Which You have wrought for those who take refuge in You,
Before the sons of men!

—Ps. 31:19

We all have personal changes, some joyous and some painful. We also have governmental changes that affect us, including safety issues, terrorists, laws, and new leaders. We fear opposition, war, and unsettled disputes in the Middle East and other nations that would disrupt our nation. The media create confusion and distrust. We surrender to the anxiety and feel as if we are in a sea of lies, caught up in the waves as we struggle to stay afloat.

Then I am reminded by His Word that His promises and His grace are sufficient. In our weakness, His strength is made perfect. In Him, believers have refuge. We can know He is with us by His divine peace in the toughest trials. It's our choice to receive all He has for us and live in love, peace, joy, patience, kindness, goodness, faithfulness, gentleness, and self-control through the Holy Spirit who dwells within us.

Psalm 112:1–10 tells of the prosperity of the one who fears the Lord. Verse 10 tells the result: *"The wicked will see it and be vexed, / He will gnash his teeth and melt away; / The desire of the wicked will perish."*

Pray for our nation, for God's hedge of protection to surround His people, here and around the world. Pray for God to soften the heart of the enemy so there will be peace. Pray that all God's children will bow before Him in awe as the enemy perishes. The Lord *is* for us, so who can be against us? Jesus shed His blood on the cross and paid the ultimate sacrifice for our eternal life. Rejoice, for this is the day the Lord has made. Let us rejoice and be glad in it as we strive to make the personal changes that help us walk closer to Him, as a light upon the hill.

God's Word: Food for Thought

God's Word explains the idea of being fit and eating healthily so our bodies, His temple, are beautiful and healthy and pleasing to God. Read Romans 14:1–23, a passage in which Paul teaches the principles of conscience (one man has faith that he may eat all things, but he who is weak eats vegetables only). Then read 1 Timothy 4:1–5. Genesis 1:29 says, *"Then God said, 'Behold, I have given you every plant yielding seed that is on the surface of all the earth, and every tree which has fruit yielding seed; it shall be food for you.'"*

Health from a Biblical Viewpoint

How does the Bible view health, and what principles does it contain for healthy living? Our eternal Father wants us to be healthy. *"Beloved, I pray that in all respects you may prosper and be in good health, just as your soul prospers"* (3 John 2). But many today, even believers, abuse their bodies. Others become health-food fanatics. But both may not be healthy and both could suffer illness.

What is the true biblical approach to health? Surprisingly, the Bible gives a few remedies for sickness. Primarily, it lays out a way of life that, if followed, will prevent diseases.

Bible Remedies

1. Strong drink is prescribed for those ready to perish: *"Give strong drink to him who is perishing, / And wine to him whose life is bitter. / Let him drink and forget his poverty / And remember his trouble no more"* (Prov. 31:6–7).

2. *"No longer drink water exclusively, but use a little wine for the sake of your stomach and your frequent ailments"* (1 Tim. 5:23).
3. Isaiah made a fig poultice to alleviate a deadly boil on King Hezekiah in 2 Kings 20:1–7.

Healing Ministries

1. Healing belongs to Almighty God, our Healer (Exod. 15:26; Jer. 30:17, 33:6).
2. He promises freedom from disease for those who diligently obey all His statutes. His teaching servants also have a healing ministry to perform. The Levites were guardians of the general health of the Israelites (Lev 13).
3. The Levites had to be without blemish and in good health (Lev. 21:9–11, 16–24).
4. The people knew to consult priests and prophets, not doctors, when illness occurred (1 Kings 14:1–5 [Abijah]; 1 Kings 17:17–24 [Elijah]; 2 Kings 4:18–35 [Elisha]).
5. Our Savior performed many works of healing in His public ministry, even using natural substances as Isaiah did (John 9:1–7).
6. Healing others and teaching the laws of health are vital to the Great Commission for disciples in every age (Mark 16:15–18).
7. Luke was called the beloved physician (Col. 4:14), indicating that he was noted for a healing ministry as a doctor, a vessel for God's purpose of healing.

Obedience Is the Key to Health

Some people believe health foods and vitamins are the key to health. Others say herbs. Still others name a special exercise or massage. These may, indeed, have much value, but the real key to health is often overlooked. Obeying all the laws of God is the only way to health and happiness.

1. We are promised good health for obedience to all of God's laws (Exod. 15:26, Deut. 28:1–14).
2. The curse for disobedience is poor health and sickness (Deut. 28:15–62).

Biblical Laws of Health

There are many direct biblical laws and principles of health that we should follow. Here are some of the direct biblical laws of health:

1. The primary biblical law of health is often ignored or neglected by many professed believers. It lays the foundation for every other biblical principle relating to the care of the human body. Simply stated, our body is the temple of the Holy Spirit, given to us by God, and is not our own to do with as we please. Our Savior paid a great price to buy us as His own. Therefore, we ought to glorify the Almighty in our body and spirit (1 Cor. 6:19-20). Every part of our body should be used for the glory of God.

2. The law of clean and unclean flesh foods is another major biblical health law. Certain animals, birds, fish, and other creatures were never created to be eaten. Noah knew about clean and unclean animals (Gen. 7:1-3). The laws of the clean and unclean in Leviticus 11 and Deuteronomy 14:1-20 were not just laws for Israel. They have been in effect for all humankind at all times. We are not to eat unclean foods but are to be a holy people.

3. Other things not to eat include the following: anything that dies of itself (Deut. 14:21), a young goat cooked in its mother's milk (Deut. 14:21; Exod. 23:19), blood or improperly bled animals (Lev. 17:10-16), or fat (Lev. 3:17).

4. We are not to be drunkards and gluttons (Prov. 23:20-21, 25:16). Most people in affluent societies eat and drink too much. Scientific evidence has proved that being overweight increases mortality from diabetes, digestive diseases, and coronary disease. Most authorities agree that overeating and underactivity cause 95 percent of obesity.

5. Ask the Lord to heal you if you become sick (James 5:14-15). Your faith in the power of the Almighty and His promises to heal you makes you whole (Matt. 9:20-22).

6. Maintain a truly joyful spirit. You accomplish that by producing the fruit of the Holy Spirit (Gal. 5:22-23) and living by every word of God (Matt. 4:4, Prov. 17:22, 14:30, 4:20-22).

7. Be an active person. That means a lot of physical work, which may include exercise and sports (Prov. 6:6–11, 10:4–5, 12:11, 20:13, 19:15, 14:23; 1 Tim. 4:7–8).
8. Get proper sleep and rest. Exodus 20:8–11 is a health law as well as a spiritual law. He gives His beloved sleep (Ps. 4:8, 127:1–2; Eccles. 5:12).
9. Eat food grown in good soil. Try to obtain or grow your own high-quality food. Luke 13:6–9, Proverbs 28:19, Deuteronomy 14:22–23, and many other passages show that biblical laws are based on God's ideal agricultural society. In today's industrialism, it's difficult to get into harmony with God's ways, but we ought to do the best we can, with His help.
10. Keep your inner body clean and fast occasionally for both spiritual and physical health. Isaiah 52:11, 2 Corinthians 7:1, and I John 3:3 refer to both physical and spiritual cleanliness. Fasting is a way to cleanse your body internally (Isa. 58:6–8). Balm of Gilead (which can be purchased today) is a digestive cleanser (Jer. 8:22). Bathing in running water is a biblical prescription for cleanliness (Lev. 15:13, 2 Kings 5:10).

Proper Perspective on Food

In 1 Corinthians 6:9–20, we see that we should not do anything that isn't good for us, whether or not the Bible expressly forbids it. Even if we're allowed to eat something, we should not do so if we cannot control how much we eat. The Almighty has given us an appetite for food and stomachs to digest it, but that doesn't mean we should delve into gluttony or take in something that is harmful to our bodies.

Some will say, "Oh well! Everything is bad for us to some extent, so why get so picky?" They may even use Mark 7:14–23 or Romans 14:17 to justify a casual disregard for what they eat. The proper perspective on food and drink is expressly stated in 1 Corinthians 10:31: *"Whether, then, you eat or drink or whatever you do, do all to the glory of God."* Let us wholeheartedly serve Him in all things.

Living Water

Two-thirds of our body is water. Nothing is more vital to health than pure water. Natural spring or well water is a blessing from God. So much of the world is sick because of impure water. Waterborne diseases plague the poorer nations. Human-made pollutants added or dumped into water systems are responsible for untold deaths and misery. Pray God's blessings over your well and over the place you receive water.

Avoid Unclean Foods

If we profess to live by every Word of God and believe that Leviticus 11 and Deuteronomy 14 apply to us, then let's be honest. Otherwise, why bother? It takes diligence to obey God. Let's not play Russian roulette with our food intake. Does that mean that when we're at someone's house or in a restaurant we should make a spectacle of ourselves? Of course not! There is a way of being very discreet and finding out quietly what to avoid. At a friend's home or at a gathering, simply avoid anything questionable. In the case of close friends, tell them very politely about your beliefs. That way, you won't feel apprehensive and unable to enjoy yourself.

Some may point to 1 Timothy 4:4–5, which says, *"For everything created by God . . . is sanctified by means of the word of God and prayer,"* or 1 Corinthians 10:25, which says, *"Eat anything that is sold in the meat market without asking questions for conscience' sake,"* to prove that we shouldn't carefully examine what we ingest. After all, in public, it may be a little embarrassing. It is easy to eat biblically in quiet, good taste without causing a scene if a person really wants to obey God.

When we ask God to bless our food for the nourishment of our bodies, we do not sanctify something that is impure or unclean. We come before God, giving thanks for the good food He has given us. We must do our part to ensure that it's healthy and nutritious, or our prayer is meaningless. We ask the Almighty to do what we cannot do: to bestow His blessing and remove impurities that we are unaware of or cannot do anything about.

In Acts 10:9–15, we read that Peter was on the housetop praying and became hungry. He fell into a trance and saw the sky open, and a great sheet came down filled with all kinds of four-footed animals and crawling creatures of the earth and birds of the sky. Verses 13–15 tell us that Peter heard a voice tell him, *"Get up, Peter, kill and eat!"* Peter responded, *"By no means, Lord, for I have never eaten anything unholy and unclean."* And a voice spoke to him again, *"What God has cleansed, no longer consider unholy."*

The Bread of Life
Bread is the staff of life (Lev. 26:26, Ezek. 4:16–17), yet so many Sabbath-keepers have neglected wholesome bread, the foundation of good health, as a basic part of their diets. Bread strengthens people's hearts (Ps. 104:15).

Some people say they don't like the taste of wholesome food. Our very own taste buds have in many cases become perverted. If you have the will to obey God Almighty, He can change your tastes, thoughts, and actions.

Sugar or Honey?
The Bible shows us the proper sweetener to use: honey. We are even told to eat it, especially the honeycomb (Prov. 24:13), but only in moderation (Prov. 25:16, 27). When you use honey instead of sugar, you will need less sweetener.

Honey that is raw and locally harvested would be the honey used in scripture.

Herbs for Service
The Creator placed Adam and Eve in a garden and told them to dress and keep it. He gave us every herb-bearing seed and every tree with fruit-bearing seed to be our food (Gen. 1:29–31). Further instruction must have come at that time, but it is not recorded in the Bible. At the time of Noah, the Almighty specified that

clean animals were also for our food (compare Genesis 9:1–4 with Genesis 7:2).

Herbs are the foundation of humans' diets. Meat, milk, and honey are accessories. Cereal grains are a good basic herb (plant-bearing seed). Just as grass was made for cattle, so herbs were made for the service of humans (Ps. 104:14–15). Oils such as those made from olives, sunflowers, and corn make our faces shine in health. The life-giving herbs mentioned in the Bible are not our quick-fed, artificially fertilized, sprayed, processed, and packaged vegetables. They are the crops grown on healthy soil, eaten raw or lightly steamed, properly processed, if at all. Biblical herbs are also the plants that one gathers from the mountains (Prov. 27:25). Most people today are either too busy or too lazy to gather crops from the countryside or plant their own (Prov. 10:5). As we sow in our bodies, so shall we reap.

Milk and Cheese

When our Savior described the land of promise, He called it a land flowing with milk and honey. The Bible uses this phrase 17 times to describe a land of plenty and good things.

The Bible mentions butter made from cow and sheep milk (Deut. 32:14). Goat milk is especially prized (Prov. 27:26–27). Milk is a very mild substance compared to meat (1 Pet. 2:2, 1 Cor. 3:2, Heb. 5:12–13). That brings us to a controversial subject: eating milk and meat together. Exodus 23:19, 34:26, and Deuteronomy 14:21 tell us not to boil a young goat in its mother's milk. That could mean not to eat a young goat that is still nursing from its mother. That is probably the true meaning, for in Genesis 18:8, we find that Abraham took butter and milk and a calf to feed the Lord God.

The Bible shows that cow's milk is made into butter (Isa. 7:21–22) or cheese (2 Sam. 17:29, 1 Sam. 17:18). Goat's milk has unusual properties, making it easy to digest, even curing some stomach ulcers.

Is milk only for children? Not according to the Bible, which is written from the Middle Eastern point of view. As Smith's Bible Dictionary says,

> As an article of diet, milk holds a more important position in eastern countries than with us. It is not a mere adjunct in cookery, or restricted to the use of the young, although it is naturally the characteristic food of childhood, both from its simple and nutritive qualities. (1 Peter 2:2) and particularly as contrasted with meat, (1 Corinthians 3:2; Hebrews 5:12) but beyond this it is regarded as substantial food adapted alike to all ages and classes. Not only the milk of cows, but of sheep, (32:14) of camels, (Genesis 32:15) and of goats, (Proverbs 27:27) was used; that latter appears to have been most highly prized.[1]

Drink the Pure Blood of the Grape

The Bible is not silent on the topic of wine. Drunkenness is condemned, but the right use of wine and even strong drink is not only recommended, it is commanded.

Our Savior lived a pure, clean, and sinless life. He would not damage His own body or anyone else's. He drank wine and even changed water into wine. The apostle Paul, who taught us in 1 Corinthians 6:19–20 to glorify the Almighty with our bodies, prescribed wine to Timothy for a stomach ailment in 1 Timothy 5:23. Notice that he said "a little wine." There is a right use of wine. Wine is a blessing from God for keeping His laws (Deut. 14:22–26).

As is so often the case, humans pervert what God gives as a blessing. Wine as a health-giving beverage is especially important for the elderly. It has a blessing associated with it if used properly. Wine helps us to be joyful (Ps. 104:14–15). Use it properly.

---

1. "Milk," *Smith's Bible Dictionary*, https://www.biblestudytools.com/dictionaries/smiths-bible-dictionary/milk.html.

Fasting to Loose the Bonds of Sin

There is certainly a tie between the physical and the spiritual. Nowhere is this tie more clear than with fasting, a physical and spiritual act that should produce a spiritual and physical benefit.

At times, we drift away from God and His ways. Unrepented sins and poisonous thoughts get the upper hand and lead us to spiritual sickness, resulting in God not hearing our prayers (Isa. 59:1-2). Bodily poisons from sinful eating habits or wrong thoughts can build up and make us physically sick. The biblical prescription in both cases is fasting. Primarily, fasting has a spiritual purpose. It should loose the bonds of wickedness and draw us closer to God, undoing the heavy burdens of sin and making us aware of the needs of the poor (Isa. 58:1-7). It has both a spiritual and physical blessing. Done the right way, God says, *"Then your light will break out like the dawn, / And your recovery will speedily spring forth; / ... Then you will call, and the Lord will answer"* (Isa. 58:8-9).

Keeping the Sabbath Holy

Isaiah 58:13-14 gives another key to health: keeping the Sabbath holy. In this world of turmoil, nervous tension, and striving to make a living, we need a haven of rest. The Sabbath can be a time of spiritual and physical rejuvenation to recharge and tackle the responsibility of life for the next week. Properly kept, the Sabbath is essential to spiritual and physical health.

Other Biblical Health Principles

I hope that all who seek to obey God will look to the Bible as the foundation of all knowledge and follow its guiding principles. The Bible provides a way of life and affects what we do, say, think, wear, and eat.

In faith, as well as in health, some people will exhibit initial enthusiasm but then lapse into their old ways. Like the seed that fell on stony ground, they joyfully begin to follow the biblical laws of health, but when difficulty or other adverse conditions come, they give up. Living by the Bible, including its laws of health, is not a game but rather a lifetime vocation. Everyone needs improvement in their physical and spiritual lives, which requires diligence and continual effort.

Look to the Bible for guidelines. The Bible discusses foods such as cucumbers, melons, leeks, onions, garlic (Num. 11:5), myrrh, aloe, spices, and so much more. Use these Bible foods and substances. Learn more about your body, the temple of the Holy Spirit. Treat it with respect. Teach others to do the same.

The Almighty God, our Healer Jehovah Rapha, is and always has been concerned about our health. Jesus said, *"If you love Me, you will keep My commandments"* (John 14:15) (see also John 14:21, 23; John 15:10; 1 John 5:3). These verses pertain to all commandments, not just what we eat. We are expected to try to do good to show Him our respect and love for all He has done for us.

It is wise to follow God's Word concerning all matters. All the information He gave us was for our better and healthier life on earth. Jesus came that we might have a more abundant life. It's our choice.

Love

Agape (ἀγάπη) is love in a spiritual sense. The term *s'agapo* (Σ'αγαπώ), which means "I love you" in ancient Greek, often refers to unconditional love rather than attraction, as suggested by *eros* (the root of the English word *erotic*). *Agape* is selfless; it gives and expects nothing in return. It is used in 1 Corinthians 13, the love chapter of the Bible, and described there and throughout the New Testament as brotherly love, affection, good will, love, and benevolence. *Agape* also denotes feelings for children or a spouse. It indicates contentment with and high regard for someone else. It's the unconditional love of God for His children. Thomas Aquinas explained it as "to will the good of another."

Eros (ἔρως) is physical, passionate love with sensual desire and longing. It's romantic, pure emotion without the balance of logic; it's love at first sight. The modern Greek word *erotas* means intimate love. It can apply to dating relationships as well as marriage. Plato refined the definition, saying that although one may initially feel *eros* toward another, with contemplation, the feeling becomes appreciation for the person's beauty. Plato does not talk of physical attraction as a necessary part of love; hence the word *platonic*, which means without physical attraction. In *Symposium*, the most famous ancient work on the subject, Plato urges Socrates to argue that *eros* helps the soul recall knowledge of beauty and contributes to an understanding of spiritual truth, the ideal form of youthful beauty that leads us to feel erotic desire. He suggests that even sensual love aspires to the non-corporeal, spiritual plane of existence because finding its truth, just like finding any truth, leads to transcendence. Lovers and philosophers are inspired to seek truth through the means of *eros*.

Philia (φιλία) is brotherly love. In both ancient and modern Greek, it refers to an affectionate regard or friendship. This type of love has give and take. It is a dispassionate, virtuous love, a concept developed by Aristotle. In his work *Nicomachean Ethics*, he expresses *philia* variously as loyalty to friends, family, lovers, and community. It requires virtue, equality, and familiarity.

Storge (στοργή) indicates affection in ancient and modern Greek. It is natural affection, like that felt by parents for offspring. Rarely used in ancient works, it almost exclusively describes relationships within the family. It also expresses mere acceptance or putting up with situations, as in loving the tyrant.

Some feel love more easily than others, and some don't feel love at all. We are all different, but Jesus commands us, "A new commandment I give to you, that you love one another: *just as I have loved you, you also are to love one another*. By this all people will know that you are my disciples, if you have love for one another" (John 13:34–35 emphasis added).

It's easy to talk about love and harder to act on it. How often do we become angry, lose patience with, or dislike someone because he or she is different, doesn't agree with us, or gets on our nerves? How often does that turn to hatred or ill feelings?

How do we react toward others of different denominations or religions, terrorists, criminals, corrupt leaders, gangs, singers, and actors portraying evil ways?

Jesus gave us the ultimate example when He forgave the criminal on the cross beside Him. Christ did not approve of the man's sin, but He loved him because of his faith and told him that he would join Him in paradise that very day. The man believed in Christ and had a love in his heart for Jesus for his salvation. We never know who will turn to Jesus because of the example we have set through our love.

We must be an example of God's love for us as described in John 3:16: *"For God so loved the world, that He gave His only begotten Son, that whoever believes in Him shall not perish, but have eternal life."* He describes love in 1 Corinthians 13:4–7. If we fall short of that description, we are ignoring our Lord and His will, allowing the evil one to win. In Matthew 5:44, Jesus tells us to pray for our enemies. That is a tall order, but when we walk in the light of Christ, love becomes easier.

When they crucified Christ, He said, *"Father, forgive them; for they do not know what they are doing"* (Luke 23:34). That is Christ's example for us to follow. He prayed for His enemies. When we know our Lord, we can love with an *agape* love. In John 14:15, Jesus tells us, *"If you love Me, you will keep My commandments."*

When we learn to lay aside our differences and dislikes for one another, when we learn how to love without judgment, when we learn how to pray in a loving spirit, when we are capable of separating ourselves from those with wrong desires or evil ways, when we learn to be more like Christ with love in our hearts for everyone, we will truly be walking in His light. I am working on this, and I pray that all will come to share His *agape* love. Love does conquer all.

Thorn in His Flesh

Because of the surpassing greatness of the revelations, for this reason, to keep me from exalting myself, there was given me a thorn in the flesh, a messenger of Satan to torment me—to keep me from exalting myself! Concerning this I entreated the Lord three times that it might leave me. And He has said to me, "My grace is sufficient for you, for power is perfected in weakness." Most gladly, therefore, I will rather boast about my weaknesses, so that the power of Christ may dwell in me. Therefore I am well content with weaknesses, with insults, with distresses, with persecutions, with difficulties, for Christ's sake; for when I am weak, then I am strong.
—2 Cor. 12:7–10

Most of us have experienced a thorn in our flesh—something or someone who irritates us to the point of making us weak, stealing our joy and peace. Paul tells us that he was given a thorn in his flesh, a messenger of satan to keep him from exalting himself.

Jesus knew that Paul the Pharisee (a religious leader who hated Jesus, had Stephen stoned, and took Christians captive) would become an obedient servant to Him. Jesus also knew that Paul would love Him and deliver His Word, for Paul's epistles comprise most of the New Testament. Jesus knew Paul's flesh, that he would fall subject to exalting himself. Like us all, the apostle Paul struggled against his sinful nature. In 2 Corinthians 12:8, Paul says he asked the Lord three times to make the thorn depart from him, but Jesus did not. Sometimes, we are better off weak, humbled in His sight so we do our services for Christ without judgment or self-exaltation. Jesus appeared to Paul and said, *"My grace is sufficient for you, for power is perfected in weakness"* (2 Cor. 12:9).

We must pray for discernment to know whether God allowed a thorn for His glory or whether satan is trying to steal our joy. Can you rely on Christ for joy to show others His power?

When I was battling cancer, my husband and I determined to rely fully on Christ. We traveled the journey with pure delight. I couldn't wait to go in for treatments, to see my new friends, and to silently lift up others there. God had given me a purpose. I was strong in Him in my weakness. Every time, through that thorn called cancer, He was there. Great and marvelous things would happen for others to see His glory, and all the time I had a smile. I was the happiest person because I had surrendered to Him for strength and knew He was with me.

I am a sinner, and as I asked for forgiveness and repented, God used me to help others. It's hard to fully understand how others feel if we haven't walked in their shoes.

Other thorns have kept me from exalting myself to show God's power. Being happy and allowing Christ to handle our problems is a great opportunity for others to see Christ through us. I am reminded of Job and what God said to satan, *"Behold, all that he has is in your power, only do not put forth your hand on him"* (Job 1:12). From there, satan tempted and tested Job's faith in a way that would destroy most people. Satan stole Job's life as he knew it, killed his family, and attempted to destroy his faith. There are ups and downs in this story, but satan does not destroy Job's faith, and God rewards Job. There are many times in our lives when satan steals from us and kills but cannot destroy our faith because we stand on the foundation, the Rock, Christ our Lord. We have the opportunity to rely on Christ for strength, to allow His love to shine through us for others to see, and to not lose hope. That is the abundant life Christ came to give us—that even in the lowest or most troublesome moments, we can have peace, joy, and love through Him who loves us. Paul heard the Lord and responded that he would rather boast about his weaknesses so the power of Christ could dwell in him. Paul was content with weaknesses, insults, distresses, persecutions, and difficulties for Christ's sake. Paul said, *"When I am weak, then I am strong"* (2 Cor. 12:10).

In Philippians 4:13, Paul reminds us, *"I can do all things through Him who strengthens me."* Paul lived an abundant life, even though he spent time in prison and died a martyr. He lived a life full of love, compassion, and joy, cherishing the faith he had in his eternal life because he lived for Christ.

When we endure hardships, insults, distresses, and persecutions for Christ's sake with joy, we reveal the light of Christ to others. There are so many factors in this world—some people are rich, and some are rulers, community leaders, doctors, and county workers. Some work in fields, schools, organizations, and homes, while some are bedridden, frail from disease, cold, and hungry. Some are ministers and teachers of His Word. Life is not about the positions we hold but rather our faith in God and the joy we have in the position we hold. That is why Christ said in Matthew 19:30, *"But many who are first will be last; and the last, first."*

Paul, John, Luke, Matthew, Mark, Peter, and all the others who suffered thorns in the flesh could endure abundantly with joy, love, and strength through Christ while spreading His Word. They will be first in the eternal kingdom of our heavenly Father. Will you be first or last? This has nothing to do with your salvation but everything to do with your abundant life in Christ. Jesus said, "The thief comes only to steal and kill and destroy; I came that they may have life, and have *it* abundantly (John 10:10).

Putting the Thanks Back in Thanksgiving

Give thanks to the L*ORD*, *for he is good; for His lovingkindness is everlasting.*

—Ps. 118:1

Growing up, our home was not filled with riches, but it was filled with love from family and friends. At Thanksgiving and Christmas, we celebrated with gratefulness. My grandmother Canny who was Spirit-filled like none I have ever known, often led us in a spirit of gratitude.

Gifts under the tree were few, but the love of Christ abounded. One Christmas, I wanted a rubber foam pillow very badly, and Canny made sure I got it. I kept that pillow until it finally fell apart not too many years ago. Over the years, we were blessed with more money, and the gifts became so abundant that they consumed the room. By the time I had my own grandkids, there were so many gifts that they tired of opening them. That had to change. Now gifts no longer consume the room so the love of Christ can fill us up.

Family prayers of daily thanksgiving at the dinner table are so important. Tell the little ones and young adults about Christ and how they, too, can enjoy eternal life if they choose Christ as their Savior. I thank God for my Canny and a family that loved

Christ. I thank God for my husband and his godly family. What a witness to my son and grandchildren!

When my dad and sister went to be with our Lord, they left empty places at our Thanksgiving table. When they were alive, our table was full of family and friends. After feeling down about the holidays for a couple years, I sought the Lord, and the family opted for a change of venue. We began eating at a small country club. The large room was full of friends, and every type of food filled the buffet. Now that is our tradition. We don't make a big to-do over things but live our lives quietly with gratitude in and for all things through Christ.

I hope Thanksgiving isn't just a holiday for you. It should be a way of life for every Christian. We serve a wonderful God who sent His Son to die for us. As you reflect on what you're thankful for, remember God's blessings. Remember that this nation was a blessing to those fleeing Europe for the freedom to worship Christ the Lord.

If you're also looking at empty chairs for the holidays, allow our Lord's peace to take you through this time. Let no evil steal your joy, remembering what is of Christ and what is not. Pray for guidance by the Holy Spirit. If you feel rushed, exhausted, overwhelmed, angry, or sad, stop and fall to your knees, seeking Him who provides our peace and wisdom. I say this from experience.

Peace I leave with you; My peace I give to you; not as the world gives do I give to you. Do not let your heart be troubled, nor let it be fearful.
—John 14:27

Do not let your heart be troubled; believe in God, believe also in Me.
—John 14:1

Encouragement

Paul wrote the letter to the Philippians while he was in prison. He was troubled by other Christian workers who opposed him and was distressed by false teachings in the church at Philippi. Sound familiar?

Philippians is an encouragement and a reminder that our lives in Christ are a gift of God's grace, blessed with joy and peace that we have received through faith. *"I press on toward the goal for the prize of the upward call of God in Christ Jesus"* (Phil. 3:14).

The first chapter of Philippians reminds us that we must pray for others: ministers of Christ, church leaders and teachers, missionaries, godly friends, Christians around the world, and especially believers in our homes, states, and nation.

Paul and Timothy, bond-servants of Christ Jesus,

To all the saints in Christ Jesus who are in Philippi, including the overseers and deacons: Grace to you and peace from God our Father and the Lord Jesus Christ.

I thank my God in all my remembrance of you, always offering prayer with joy in my every prayer for you all, in view of your participation in the gospel from the first day until now. For I am confident of this very thing, that He who began a good work in you will perfect it until the day of Christ Jesus. For it is only right for me to feel this way about you all, because I have you in my heart, since both in my imprisonment and in the defense and confirmation of the gospel, you all are partakers of grace with me. For God is my witness, how I long for you all with the affection of Christ Jesus. And this I pray, that your love may abound still more and more in real

knowledge and all discernment, so that you may approve the things that are excellent, in order to be sincere and blameless until the day of Christ; having been filled with the fruit of righteousness which comes through Jesus Christ, to the glory and praise of God.
—Phil. 1:1–11 emphasis added

Paul's Chains Advance the Gospel

What an example for us! Think about your life. How often have you felt as if you were in chains, and how have you responded?

Now I want you to know, brethren, that my circumstances have turned out for the greater progress of the gospel, so that my imprisonment in the cause of Christ has become well known throughout the whole praetorian guard and to everyone else, and that most of the brethren, trusting in the Lord because of my imprisonment, have far more courage to speak the word of God without fear. Some, to be sure, are preaching Christ even from envy and strife, but some also from good will; the latter do it out of love, knowing that I am appointed for the defense of the gospel; the former proclaim Christ out of selfish ambition rather than from pure motives, thinking to cause me distress in my imprisonment. What then? Only that in every way, whether in pretense or in truth, Christ is proclaimed; and in this I rejoice.

Yes, and I will rejoice, for I know that this will turn out for my deliverance through your prayers and the provision of the Spirit of Jesus Christ, according to my earnest expectation and hope, that I will not be put to shame in anything, but that with all boldness, Christ will even now, as always, be exalted in my body, whether by life or by death.

For to me, to live is Christ and to die is gain. But if I am to live on in the flesh, this will mean fruitful labor for me; and I do not know which to choose. But I am hard-pressed from both directions, having the desire to depart and be with Christ, for that is very much better; yet to remain on in the flesh is more necessary for your sake. Convinced of this, I know that I will remain and continue with you all for your progress and joy in the faith, so that your proud confidence in me may abound in Christ Jesus through my coming to you again.

—Phil. 1:12–26

Life Worthy of the Gospel

This Word is for all of us, not just Philippi. His Word is instruction, a guideline for every generation.

Only conduct yourselves in a manner worthy of the gospel of Christ, so that whether I come and see you or remain absent, I will hear of you that you are standing firm in one spirit, with one mind striving together for the faith of the gospel; in no way alarmed by your *opponents—which is a sign of destruction for them, but of salvation for you, and that too, from God. For to you it has been granted for Christ's sake, not only to believe in Him, but also to suffer for His sake, experiencing the same conflict which you saw in me, and now hear* to be *in me.*

—Phil. 1:27–30

The Word of God is filled with examples of His love, instruction, patience, and blessings for us. His Word is for every generation to follow for an abundant life on earth through Christ.

Romans

For the wages of sin is death, but the free gift of God is eternal life in Christ Jesus, our Lord.

—Rom. 6:23

Have we Christians in this free land become tolerant of sin to avoid being judgmental, unfair, unloving, selfish, or boring? Have we become intolerant to the Word of God and what it says about sin? Should we not repent and care enough about God and others to stand up against sin, the devil himself?

Has this nation become like the great Roman Empire, accepting sin and passing immoral laws that allow us to be happily sinful for the sake of not hurting feelings or being deemed socially incorrect?

We must learn how to love the person and hate the sin. Are we still America built upon the Rock, or are we Rome built upon the evils of satan? What do our new laws tell us we are? Are so-called Christian leaders acting upon God's Word or falsely using God's Word to propel them into the evils of power, greed, and self-gain? Brothers and sisters in Christ, I challenge you to repent and pray daily for our nation and our government officials; ask God to forgive us as a nation and bring this nation back to one nation under God, under His control. May our nation strive to serve the one true God, Jehovah, God Almighty in heaven, through Christ our risen Lord and Savior. Know His Word. Faith comes by hearing, and hearing comes through the Word of Christ (Rom. 10:17).

Armor of God

Put on the armor of God (Eph. 6:10–19) because satan is battling. Lucifer was called the morning star, a beautiful angel loved by God. But believing that he could rise above God, lucifer became proud, and God cast him down from heaven (Isa. 14). Now he is called satan, a name meaning accuser and adversary; he is the devil, a slanderer, one who causes division. In Arabic, the word *satan* means he-goat. Satan works hard accusing, tempting, dividing, and slandering us before God. I imagine him telling God, "Look, all I have to do is this or that, and they yield under my temptation."

I resent satan slandering me. But his slander does him no good. God judges us by our hearts, and Jesus died conquering sin. Through this victory, we should strive to please our God and be on guard against the enemy at all times. We have great power through the Holy Spirit to cast out satan so he can't tempt us, but do we use that power? We need the Helper, the Holy Spirit that God our Father sent us, Who is available every minute of every day. Jesus ascended to heaven to sit at the right hand of God the Father, but He left us His Holy Spirit so we would not have to fend for ourselves (John 16:7).

Satan works with his band of angels (better known as demons), attempting to destroy all that God our Father loves, all that He created for His pleasure. Satan starts with the church body, causing dissension. Dissension causes separation, division, and wasted time to rebuild. We must pray in the Spirit, rebuking satan from our presence and hearing God, praying for His blessings and protection so we can serve Him through the power of the Holy Spirit, giving all glory to Him who loves us.

Satan works hard to destroy the family. When we are sidetracked as a family, we cannot serve God with our whole beings. Satan orders his demons to sidetrack us in order to steal our joy, kill our spirits, and destroy our relationships with God. He wants to keep the unsaved from Christ—the ultimate destruction (John 10:10).

Do you see demons working in your life? Consider these schemes from satan:

1. Keep them busy, tired, and weary, doing all the non-essential things, especially on the Sabbath, so they have no time for God. Work them long hours to maintain empty lifestyles.
2. Give them desires for unhealthy things, gross lusts for all the evil I possess. Give them a tongue that speaks filthy words so their temple becomes an unsightly place for the Holy Spirit to dwell in.
3. Make them overspend and fall into debt so they can't give to God or care for their families.
4. Discourage healthy family time so they have problems and disorder in the home.
5. Overstimulate their minds with TV, computers, and phones so they can't hear God speaking to them.
6. Keep their tables full of magazines and books so they have no desire to read the Bible.
7. Keep their mailboxes full of sweepstakes to get rich quick and chase after material things instead of desiring the good things God offers them.
8. Show them glamorous and sexual models that will ultimately make them dissatisfied with their own appearances and spouses.
9. Keep couples too exhausted for physical intimacy so they look elsewhere for satisfaction.
10. Emphasize Santa and the Easter Bunny so they do not spread the true meaning of these holidays.
11. Keep them involved in good causes so they have no time to enhance the eternal ones.

12. Make them self-sufficient, working in their own strength so they do not allow God's strength to work in them.
13. Blind their eyes, deafen their ears, and close their minds to the understanding of God's Word and the lifestyle He wants for them. Teach them how to justify their wrongs and avoid responsibility. Make them all follow me, satan, and forsake the Creator.

Even satan knows God is the Almighty, the First and the Last, the Creator of all, the one true God. Because he knows, he's desperately seeking to devour all he can. He messed up, and he wants us to mess up, too. But fear not! We have Jesus, His Word, His Holy Spirit, and the armor of God.

If you're exhausted, fearful, ill, restless, unable to sleep, ill-tempered, dissatisfied with yourself or those around you, desiring things or ungodly lifestyles, quarrelsome, too angry to pray, or unable to love your enemy (1 Sam. 26:18–21, Job 31:29–30, Rom. 12:20, Luke 6:27, Matt. 6:12–15, Luke 23:34), you may be under satan's yolk (B.U.S.Y.).

Put on the armor of God. Use that sword, the Word of God. To use it, you must know it. Hold up that shield, your faith, to deflect satan's darts, resisting his temptations. Shod your feet with the gospel of peace, standing firmly on the Word. Wear the breastplate to protect your heart and mind with truth, living in righteousness. And keep the helmet on to secure your salvation. We must be warriors, living securely and fearlessly in Christ, our refuge and tower of strength, against the enemy. He who loves us and created us for His pleasure will never abandon us. Rebuke satan and his band of demons in the name of Jesus and live peacefully, joyously, and greatly in the abundant life that Jesus came to give. Our flesh is weak, but He is strong. Hallelujah!

Prophetic Movement

Behold, I will do something new,
Now it will spring forth;
Will you not be aware of it?
I will even make a roadway in the wilderness,
Rivers in the desert.

—Isa. 43:19

And God has appointed in the church, first apostles, second prophets, third teachers, then miracles, then gifts of healings, helps, administrations, various kinds of tongues.

—1 Cor. 12:28

But earnestly desire the greater gifts. And I show you a still more excellent way.

—1 Cor. 12:31

For now we see in a mirror dimly, but then face to face; now I know in part, but then I shall know fully just as I also have been fully known.

—1 Cor. 13:12

But now faith, hope, love, abide these three; but the greatest of these is love.

—1 Cor. 13:31

And there was a prophetess, Anna.

—Luke 2:36

Prophetic Movement

Most of us have read that women should be silent in the church; however, women should seek the Lord and serve in the Holy Spirit as God directs—just as He directed Anna. The Bible shows many examples of men and women who served God as directed by His Spirit.

The Holy Spirit leads us along a prophetic path. He will reveal hidden mysteries as we go: *"You will make known to me the path of life; / In Your presence is fullness of joy; / In Your right hand there are pleasures forevermore"* (Ps. 16:11).

God will provide us with prophetic motion. Prophetic motion is a time of spiritual movement, activity, advancement, and acceleration. The path leads us up the mountain of God. You will go higher than ever before. If we are to know God more completely, we must go higher: *"For as the heavens are higher than the earth, / So are My ways higher than your ways / And My thoughts than your thoughts"* (Isa. 55:9).

The cry of our hearts must be, *"Make me know Your ways, O Lord; / Teach me Your paths. / Lead me in Your truth and teach me, / For You are the God of my salvation; / For You I wait all the day"* (Ps. 25:4–5).

Spread your wings. *"Yet those who wait for the Lord / Will renew their strength; / They will mount up with wings like eagles, / They will run and not get tired, / They will walk and not become weary"* (Isa. 40:31). Mount up! The purpose is to go higher than you have before. It is time for elevation.

Where are you in your spiritual walk? Surely the Lord has been moving strongly in your life. Listen to the prophets of this day, for God speaks His wisdom through those gifted and those who will listen. Desire God's discernment, and you will know when you are in tune with His Holy Spirit.

The Apostles' Creed

Those who declare publicly that they belong to me, I will do the same for them before my Father in heaven.
—Matt. 10:32 GNT

The Apostles' Creed is a declaration of the Christian faith. It is used in many denominations today. This creed is not in the Bible but was derived from the apostles' teachings in the Bible. It has been passed down through the generations, for all generations, as a proclamation of faith unto the Lord. I am not saying that we must say this creed, but we must declare from the heart our faith in Christ and become born again, as taught by Jesus. This creed is a good example of how Christians in the early church publicly proclaimed their faith in Christ.

The Apostles' Creed

1. I believe in God the Father, Almighty, Maker of heaven and earth (Acts 17:24).
2. And in Jesus Christ, His only begotten Son, our Lord (John 1:18).
3. Who was conceived by the Holy Ghost, born of the Virgin Mary (Matt. 1:20–21).
4. Who suffered under Pontius Pilate, was crucified, dead and buried; He descended into hell (Matt. 27:26).
5. The third day He rose again from the dead (1 Cor. 5:4).
6. He ascended into heaven and is seated at the right hand of the Father (Acts 2:31–35).

7. From thence He shall come to judge the quick and the dead (2 Tim. 4:1).
8. I believe in the Holy Ghost (John 3:5–6).
9. I believe in the holy catholic church (Rom. 12:4–5, 1 Cor. 12:12, Eph. 4:4, Col. 1:18–24, Eph. 4:4) and the communion of saints (1 Cor. 11:17–34).
10. The forgiveness of sins (Eph. 1:7).
11. The resurrection of the body (John 11:25–26, 1 Pet. 1:3–4).
12. And the life everlasting. Amen (1 John 2:25).

The communion of saints is what each of us has in common with all other believers. We have been forgiven through His death and saved by His life (Rom. 5:10), set free from the law of sin and death (Rom. 8:2), and passed from spiritual death to eternal life (John 5:24). We are all permanently adopted as children of God by the will of God (John 1:12–13). We have become God's handiwork to do good works that He has prepared for us (Eph. 2:10), and we have all been given an eternal home in the New Jerusalem in the presence of our Lord (Rev. 21:22–27). These are only a few of the blessings we have in common with all other believers.

When we say that we believe in the holy catholic church, we are confessing that Jesus Christ is the church's one holy, sacred, all-embracing foundation, that all who truly trust in Him as Savior and Lord are, by God's grace, members of this church, and that the gates of hell shall never prevail against it. *Catholic* here refers not to a denomination but to the universal church of Christ.

Followers of Christ are baptized, as taught by Christ, and exhorted by Peter following Christ's ascension into heaven and the bestowing of the Holy Spirit (Acts 2:38–42). These verses are important to observe and follow, to pass down through the generations for all to hear the salvation of Christ:

> *Peter said to them, "Repent, and each of you be baptized in the name of Jesus Christ for the forgiveness of your sins; and you will receive the gift of the Holy Spirit. For the promise is for you and your children*

and for all who are far off, as many as the Lord our God will call to Himself." And with many other words he solemnly testified and kept on exhorting them, saying, "Be saved from this perverse generation!" So then, those who had received his word were baptized; and that day there were added about three thousand souls. They were continually devoting themselves to the apostles' teaching and to fellowship, to the breaking of bread and to prayer.

—Acts 2:38–42

Notice the order:
1. Hear the call.
2. Choose salvation through belief in Christ or choose damnation in eternal fire.
3. Receive salvation by believing: "For by grace you have been saved through faith; and that not of yourselves, *it is* the gift of God" (Eph. 2:8).
4. Be baptized in water.
5. Receive the Holy Spirit, our Helper.
6. Spend time learning His Word.
7. Take part in Christian fellowship, sharing meals and prayers, proclaiming your faith publicly (Matt. 10:32).

Prayer: Part 2

As we come to believe, we realize daily prayer and constant communication with our Lord is a vital part of our lives as Christians. Below are passages that teach us how we should pray and maintain communication with Him.

The Different Types of Prayers
1. Secret – Jesus said, *"But you, when you pray, go into your inner room, close your door and pray to your Father who is in secret, and your Father who sees what is done in secret will reward you"* (Matt. 6:6).
2. Family – Cornelius was *"a devout man and one who feared [respected] God with all his household, and gave many alms [money, food, or other donations given to the poor or needy; anything given as charity] to the Jewish people and prayed to God continually. . . . Cornelius said, 'Four days ago to this hour, I was praying in my house during the ninth hour; and behold, a man stood before me in shining garments, and he said, "Cornelius, your prayer has been heard and your alms have been remembered before God"'* (Acts 10:2, 30–31).
3. Group – *"For where two or three have gathered together in My name, I am there in their midst"* (Matt. 18:20).
4. Public – *"For if I pray in a tongue, my spirit prays, but my mind is unfruitful. What is the outcome then? I will pray with the spirit and I will pray with the mind also; I will sing with the spirit and I will sing with the mind also. Otherwise if you bless in the spirit only, how will the one who fills the place of the ungifted say the 'Amen' at your giving of thanks, since he does not know what*

you are saying? For you are giving thanks well enough, but the other person is not edified" (1 Cor. 14:14–17). Paul was gifted with multilingual abilities and could pray in the tongues of the people present and also give translations as needed. If he could not translate, what good would he be to those who could not understand him? Seek your Bible for more instruction on public prayers (Acts 12:12, Matt. 14:19, James 5:16, Rom. 8:26, Luke 18:10–14, Matt. 6:1–34).

Personal Requirements for Prayer

1. Purity of heart – *"If I regard wickedness in my heart, the Lord will not hear"* (Ps. 66:18).
2. Belief – Jesus said, *"And all things you ask in prayer, believing, you will receive"* (Matt. 21:22).
3. In Christ's name – Jesus said, *"Whatever you ask in My name, that will I do, so that the Father may be glorified in the Son"* (John 14:13).
4. According to God's will – *"And this is the confidence which we have before Him, that if we ask anything according to His will, He hears us"* (1 John 5:14). Pray for and with discernment. Discernment is the ability to understand what is obscure. It means you can perceive something or comprehend what the average mind does not (see Job 12:19–21). God must shed light on the human mind to help us understand truth. It is impossible to attain wisdom without God. He gives discernment or takes it away.

The Parts of Prayer

1. Adoration – *"But at the end of that period, I, Nebuchadnezzar, raised my eyes toward heaven and my reason returned to me, and I blessed the Most High and praised and honored Him who lives forever"* (Dan. 4:34).
2. Confession – *"If we confess our sins, He is faithful and righteous to forgive us our sins and to cleanse us from all unrighteousness"* (1 John 1:9). We see an example of asking God to show us our sin in Psalm 139:23–24: *"Search me, O God, and*

and tossed by the wind. For that man ought not to expect that he will receive anything from the Lord" (James 1:5–7).

3. Disobedience – *"He who turns away his ear from listening to the law, / Even his prayer is an abomination"* (Prov. 28:9). We are not bound to the law because of Christ, but we are expected to pray with a pure heart full of love for one another, our Father, and our Savior. Do not despise the law but give thanks for Jesus who came to redeem us and give us the abundant life (John 10:10).

4. Inhumanity – *"He who shuts his ear to the cry of the poor / Will also cry himself and not be answered"* (Prov. 21:13).

5. Pride – Jesus tells this story as an example of self-pride: *"The Pharisee stood and was praying this to himself: 'God, I thank You that I am not like other people: swindlers, unjust, adulterers, or even like this tax collector. I fast twice a week; I pay tithes of all that I get'"* (Luke 18:11–12).

Does God answer all prayers? Yes, but only those prayers that are according to Christ in John 15:7–11. Jesus says in verse 7, *"If you abide in Me, and My words abide in you, ask whatever you wish, and it will be done for you."* He judges us by our hearts, and He hears us (1 Sam. 16:7, Jer. 18:10).

Be faithful in praying His blessings, benefits, and protection over your children and loved ones, daily claiming all your requests before Him through the mighty name of Jesus Christ with thankfulness, love, and appreciation in your heart.

The LORD bless you, and keep you;
The LORD make His face shine on you,
And be gracious to you;
The LORD lift up His countenance on you,
And give you peace.

—Num. 6:24–26

Bless the LORD, O my soul,
And all that is within me, bless His Holy name.
Bless the LORD, O my soul,
And forget none of His benefits;

Who pardons all your iniquities;
Who heals all your diseases;
Who redeems your life from the pit;
Who crowns you with lovingkindness and compassion;
Who satisfies your years with good things,
So that your youth is renewed like the eagle.

—Ps. 103:1–5

Seek God's angels for a safety protection to stop every evil force that would come against you or your loved ones, praying for their aid in all your needs, as we are told:

Are they [angels] not all ministering spirits, sent out to render service for the sake of those who will inherit salvation?

—Heb. 1:14

The angel of the Lord encamps around those who fear Him,
And rescues them.

—Ps. 34:7

Then Satan answered the Lord, "Does Job fear God for nothing? Have you not made a hedge [of protection] about him and his house and all that he has, on every side? You have blessed the work of his hands, and his possessions have increased in the land.

—Ps. 1:9–10

www.ingramcontent.com/pod-product-compliance
Lightning Source LLC
LaVergne TN
LVHW052255070426
835507LV00035B/2914